Howdy friends and neighbors. I'm John Burrow and this is my first GardenLine book. I chose front yards because the majority of my faithful listeners call me time after time and ask about things that they need to do with their front yard. Also, *KTRH* has that *Yard of the Month* contest and this book should help everyone compete for first prize.

Gardening is probably America's favorite pastime because it's easy, it's fun, and most us own a home at one time or another. Yep, no matter how pretty and comfortable the inside of our house is, we have to accentuate it with a pleasing front yard.

Now don't you go expecting to read a scholarly bunch of words in this book. I'm a country boy and I write just about the way I talk. And as for gardening, much of what I learned is from some schooling, trial and error, information from many of you, from nursery people, and from osmosis through Bill Zak, my co-host on GardenLine.

I hope you learn a lot in this book and if I leave anything out, call and tell me about it. I'm on *KTRH GardenLine* from 10 AM until noon Monday through Friday and from 8 to 11 every Saturday morning. I enjoy answering your questions, so keep those calls coming in.

John Burrow

GARDEN BOOK 1

YOUR FRONT YARD

by

JOHN BURROW

GRASS, SHRUBS, PLANTS AND TREES

SWAN Publishing Company
New York * California * Texas

Author: John Burrow
Editor: Pete Billac
Layout Artist: Sharon Davis
Cover Designer: Glen Clark
Cover Photographer: Gary Bankhead

UPCOMING BOOKS

Book 2:   Vegetable Gardening - August 1994
Book 3:   House Plants - December 1994
Book 4:   All About Trees - March 1995

First Printing, April 1994
Copyright @ John Burrow and SWAN Publishing Company.

Library of Congress Catalog #94-065635
ISBN 0-943629-12-8

YOUR FRONT YARD is available in quantity discounts. Please address inquiries to SWAN PUBLISHING COMPANY, 126 Live Oak, Suite 100, Alvin, Texas 77511 (713) 388-2547

Printed in the United States of America

DEDICATION

To the listeners of GardenLine who made the program number one in the state of Texas and to KTRH, the most listened to radio station in the entire Southwest.

PREFACE

This book goes into every aspect of starting a front yard from scratch; with tools, layout design, soil preparation, planting of the type of grass you want, keeping out the weeds, fertilizing the yard and cutting the grass. It also explains how to beautify an existing yard.

It tells about shrubs, evergreen plants and flowers and which plant grows best and which will bloom the longest and the prettiest. In short, it tells you just about everything that you need to do to have a really attractive front yard.

We'll talk about trees too, the kind that give shade, different colored leaves and which ones to eliminate. You'll be directed where to plant these trees so their root systems won't buckle up your walk or driveway or disturb the foundation of your home.

And, of course, maintenance. We'll discuss watering, pruning, fertilizers, insecticides, fungicides, soil additives and the best way to get rid of chinch bugs, weeds, poison ivy, and fire ants, as well as visiting relatives who stay too long. Just kidding about that last part.

The author might get a little "folksy" in this text, but he writes like he talks. He can spell, he just leaves off a lot of "g's" from the end of many words when he says them. *"That don't really matter though, does it?"* big John says, giving us one of his rare, no-top-teeth-showing smiles. *"I know what I'm sayin', they know what I'm sayin' and that's all that's necessary, ain't it? Now, let's get to plantin'."*

Pete Billac
Editor and Publisher

TABLE OF CONTENTS

GardenLine, on **NEWSRADIO 740 KTRH,** airs from 10 AM until noon each weekday morning and has almost a **quarter-of-a-million** adult listeners **per day**, 25 years of age or older; 58% male and 42% female.

On Saturday, during *GardenLine's* three-hour morning show from 8 to 11, there are more than **325,000** people who tune in, 58% **female**, and 42% **male!**

A MESSAGE FROM JOHN BURROW

This book is not only a beginners guide to planning, growing and maintaining a healthy and beautiful front yard, it's for everybody, except maybe the experts.

I start off by telling you about some of the basics, but you'd be surprised how much money experienced gardeners wasted before they became experienced. Besides, those who are experts in gardening won't buy the book nohow.

Also, I'm not apologizing for the total absence of color in this book because color costs money and to keep the price around ten dollars, only the cover has color. Hope you like my picture, but if not, unlike your garden, I can't do much about my face.

No friends, this book is for what you might call "seasoned" gardeners as well as for beginners. To those of you who have gardening experience, I know you'll laugh at some of the basics I talk about because you've already made some of these mistakes, haven't you?

What I've tried to do here is to get people started on the right path in gardening but you can't learn it all from a book. After I tell you about a plant, or grass or a tree or bush or shrub or a flower, I want you to go visit your local nursery and look at these wonders of nature. I want you to see it, smell it, feel it and make up your own mind on getting it.

I'd also like to save you some money. I'll give you a step-by-step description on what to do and how to do it but you know your pocketbook better than I do and you need to decide what you can afford.

If this book seems short, same reason as the colored pictures, the cost rises. Besides this is my first book and I need things to say in my next one. But if you read this through and follow what I tell you, you'll save a bundle of money and a whole lot of time and aggravation.

I'd like you to enjoy gardening as much as I do, I suggest you do a little "homework." My plan is to tell you enough that you'll avoid making really stupid mistakes and to whet your appetite for having a beautiful front yard. The more I can advise you to visit your nursery, the more you'll learn, the more you'll understand, and the more beautiful and satisfying your garden will be.

And don't forget to listen to *GardenLine* every weekday morning from 10 till noon and early Saturday, from 8 to 11 AM. That's 740 on your dial. If you want to ask a question about any aspect of gardening, call **526-4-740.** If you have a *GTE mobile phone,* **KTRH** will pay for the entire call and you just punch in **STAR-4-740.** Long distance, **713-630-5-740.** Now, let's do get to plantin'.

John Burrow

Chapter 1

PLAN YOUR WORK - THEN WORK YOUR PLAN

NEW FRONT YARDS

Before we get too involved with plants and planting let's start off with this gardening business academically and make a sketch of your front yard. It's going to be necessary that you read this entire chapter first, maybe this whole book, then come back and begin your planning.

The first thing you do is get a sheet of white cardboard about 24 X 36 inches to start drawing on. In fact, get three or four sheets and a mighty good eraser. And while you're at it, get some graph paper too, same size if you can and if not, scotch tape some sheets together. This doesn't have to be fancy, just functional.

Then, find a long measuring tape and you stand on one side and your wife on the other with a pad and pencil (since she's the neat one) and measure the entire front yard. Mark down the distance from the curb or sidewalk to your house, from the walkway to the driveway, from one neighbor's yard to the other and put those figures on a pad.

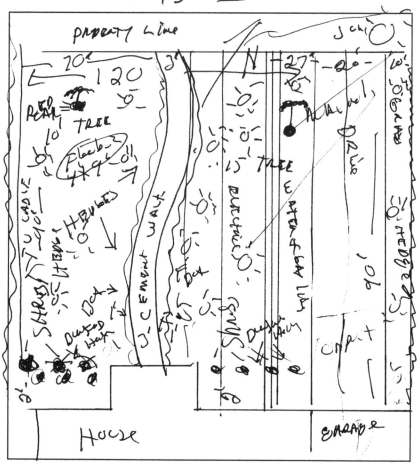

Didn't follow what I said, did you? What happened here is that you, mister do-it-by-yourself gardener, made a drawing nobody can read. Now go get your wife to help you measure and mark it off right, like I told you at first. She can't have a baby without your help and, apparently, you can't measure your front yard without her help!

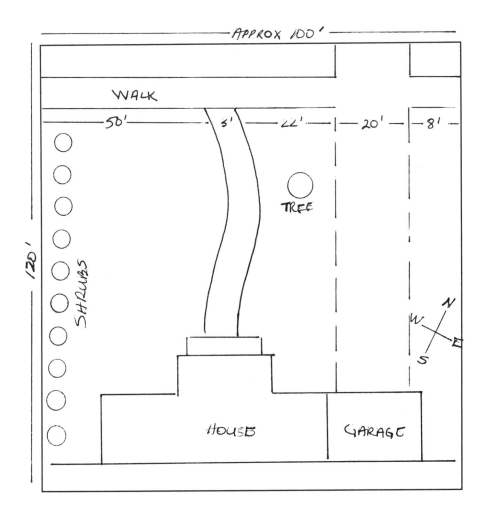

Ahh! This drawing makes more sense. Now go inside and put it down on that big sheet of paper. There's no need to be an architect or an artist to do this, just get the measurements first then get yourself a ruler and draw the lines kinda' straight on the large cardboard. A standard measurement is to make 1/4 inch equal 1 foot.

If you are *building* a house, *now* is the time to get this schematic done so you can plan your front yard the way you like it. If you're having one built for you, talk to the contractor before he gets ready for the landscaping and he stuffs in a tree or two of his choice, scatters a few plants here and there, lays sod on top of some bank sand and everything looks fine.

Well, you need to do more. In fact, you'll have most of the measurements you need on your survey sheets and/or architects plans but I'd rather you get involved and do your own measuring as well. You get the *feel* of things this way. Know what I mean? Get involved.

With new building codes, your gas, water and electric lines have to be 24 inches underground but be certain they are marked on your big sketch too. Most plants and shrubs can be planted shallow but if buy a large tree, it might go that deep so mark off where these things are before you cut into something.

POINTS TO REMEMBER WITH THIS DRAWING

1.   Mark off true North so we can see which way the sun comes up.

2.   Put in your large tree(s) and build around those.

3.   When measuring for grass or shrubs that go against your house, I like to leave some *walking space* behind them, don't push them flush against the foundation.

18

Make it easy on yourself for when you have to get behind them to cut or weed.

4.   Mark off the words *root barrier* on your diagram along the line that represents the front of your house. I'll explain more on that in a later chapter.

5.   On the graph paper, draw a rough sketch of how you *think* you want your garden to look. That extra paper and the eraser I mentioned are necessary because you'll change your mind right up to the last minute. We all do.

6.   In the event your neighbor has a large tree, spend a day watching how it might restrict the amount of sun on various parts of your lawn, you know, to give the nursery people an idea which plants will take shade and which will take sun.

RESEARCH AND LEG WORK

I know this seems like a lot of bother but trust the fact, it will be information that could make life easier for you for many years to come.

Before you actually *buy* any growing things, drive around your neighborhood and look at other yards. On weekends when you see neighbors cutting grass or digging in flower beds, why not stop and introduce yourself? People who enjoy gardening just love to tell you about their "stuff" and especially if you compliment them on it.

Ask what type of tree or bush it is in their yard that you most admire, and if they aren't certain, ask for a small clipping that you might take to your nursery and have them identify it. Maybe you can take a picture or two (or three) of their yard to take home and put in your garden sketch. They will *really* like that!

Most new neighborhoods don't have front yard fences but if you want one, talk with your neighbors on either side to see how they feel about it. If you decide on a hedge, make certain to plant it far enough on your side with sufficient room that it won't grow on your neighbor's property.

If your next door neighbors have kids who leave toys all over the place, or if their yard looks neglected, or they have an old boat parked in the driveway and they don't want you to build a fence, you might want a large "living fence" in the form of high hedges.

You also need to determine the *style* of your garden. For instance, will it be a garden of oriental plants, tropical plants, a formal garden, a "dry" garden (cactus, sand, yucca, rocks) or a contemporary garden? If you have an idea of what you'd like, this too helps the person at the plant place.

Most people plan their garden to coincide with the style of their home. To "mix and match" takes careful planning. It's not like this "eclectic" look in furnishing, with chairs and table, rugs and painting of all sorts, these can be moved by picking them up but with a garden, although you can move and transplant, it's a bit more trouble. Lot's of things to consider, aren't there?

But first, I'd mark off a spot for a tree. Then, the hedges on each side of your yard. Your next marking might be the hedges against your house. Do you know *what* you are going to plant? Again, drive your neighborhood and see what kind of healthy plants are growing in various yards. There's only half a dozen or so that are great for whichever area you're in so you can decide from these.

Friends and neighbors, make this a fun project and really, be smart about it. I know some of this seems basic but you'd be surprised at the number of people who call the program or visit their nursery trying to *describe* a certain plant or leaf or flower or bug. It's fun to listen to the first few thousand times but after that, it gets a bit trying, know what I mean?

Also, it isn't necessary to do it all at one time because regardless of how carefully you plan on paper, it will look different once it's planted and you'll want to change it time and time again. You'll see someethingn somebody else's yard and want to copy that. Or a plant that you thought would look good in this place really looks better in this other. And this is true even if you have a landscape architect design everything for you or have a professional landscape company do all the work for you.

When you decide on the plants you want, instead of planting them, just place them in various areas on *top* of the ground and back off and take a long look. Let them sit there overnight and look at them again in the morning. If they still look fine, dig the holes. If not, move them around to other locations and see if you like them the next morning.

You know, treat this placement of plants like a nasty letter you intend to write to a friend who hurt your feelings. Write the letter, insult the dickens out of them or scold them for their having offended you, then put that letter in a drawer overnight and read it again after you get a good nights rest.

Chances are, after you've slept on it and thought about it, you'll probably change your mind and make alternate plans. So when you dig these holes for plants or shrubs - trees even - before you cover them, you might want to plant something different (or say something different in that letter). This makes sense, doesn't it?

Yes, no *spur-of-the-moment* decisions in either case. That's why I say graph paper and/or an eraser because to design and plant a pleasing front yard, or to salvage a friendship, take some time and think it out. Of course, with plants, you can always dig them up and transplant them later. Again, everybody does the same thing.

There's a short cut to this business and that is if you go to your local nursery and ask them to come out and make recommendations. Most will do it for no charge, just to sell you the plants. In any event, a good sketch will help. Like Ross Perot says, "Measure **twice**, and cut **once!**"

Too, try not to make it a *job*. Enjoy it. On one of these beautiful mornings, you and your loved one drive to a local nursery and look at what they have to offer. Ma'am, you get him up early and have him take you to breakfast and then to the nursery. Or, if you both sleep in, go to the nursery and then have lunch together.

This nursery visit can be fun. Learn about these various plants and flowers, about watering and fertilizer. It's all rather simple, really. Just like a human, plants need food, water, and open air. I'm not certain about exercise. Perhaps the blades of grass get their exercise trying to dodge being stepped on by children running and playing or maybe they bend this way or that when you mow the lawn.

An item many overlook until it's too late is an *underground sprinkler system.* If you plan on having one installed, *now* is the time to do it. It's so much less of a mess than when you have an established lawn.

EXISTING FRONT YARDS

It's always a whole lot easier to *correct* that it is to *create,* yet still a challenge. And much of what I told you about New Yards can be used to change the old look you don't want to the new look you do want.

Look at other yards in your neighborhood for ideas. Draw a sketch and place the different plants and shrubs on a 24 x 36 piece of *green* cardboard (the color of most grass) and put in pictures of the plants and shrubs you would like in order to change the look you now have that you dislike.

Back off a bit and look at your tree and see if cutting a few branches will make a difference. Glance over at the long-overdue trimming of a hedge, or maybe take it out and plant something new. One new item and some pruning and shaping could change the entire look of your yard. Perhaps that Boxwood bordering your walk would look better along your house or donated to a neighbor or friend who likes it.

Maybe it's time to plant that tall-growing Red Tipped Photinia to get height or trim the sides of the ones you already have to make them grow taller because your old neighbors moved out and the new ones, well, you might not want to look into their yard for any number of reasons.

Whatever you decide to do, *plan your work - then work your plan.* Think about it, put it down on paper, look at various plants, buy them, place them where you feel they'll look the best then when you decide, dig the holes and plant.

That's why I know this book will be worth what you paid for it. I give practical advice because I hear about these mistakes all the time. If I can help you avoid many of these human errors, you'll save money and time and enjoy your garden all the more.

All you have to do is survive my cornball humor and rather *different way* of getting my various points across, and you'll do okay with planning, choosing things to plant and taking care of your front yard. So, let's get on to the next step, choosing the proper tools.

Chapter 2

GARDENING TOOLS

Buy the best tools you can afford. In fact, if you can't afford the best or near the best, save until you can. I know everybody likes a deal and many of you might shop for price but believe me, if you get "good" tools the first time, you'll probably have them for as Xlongas you have a garden. The tools you get inexpensively will last a year - maybe even two years - but you'll be replacing them again and again.

Now, What kind of tools to buy? You know you'll need the "standard" ones; a shovel, a rake and a hoe. Choose the type that *fit* you best. For instance, a strong person can get a sturdy shovel. A weaker person would choose a lighter one. Or maybe you're big and strong and still prefer a light shovel because it's easier to work with.

Go to a nearby lawn and garden center and see the tools they have to offer. Look at them, ask the price if they aren't marked, pick them up, swing them around a bit, see how well they're balanced, how they "feel" and then decide.

SHOVELS

Let's begin with the number one tool, the *shovel*. Shovels come in all shapes, sizes and weights, depending on what you plan to use them for. For instance; the all-around shovel would be the first item you'd buy. Below are a group of shovels from which you might choose.

* I never knew why some people call them shovels and some call them spades. I guess it depends on the part of the country you're from. To make certain, I looked it up in my dictionary and it seems a spade is heavier than a shovel and is mostly for scooping and cutting, whereas a shovel picks stuff up and digs. It doesn't make a difference what you call it; it's a garden tool and common sense tells you to select the one that is best for what you need to do with it.

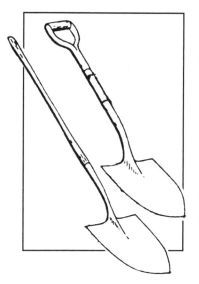

A: Garden shovel: Usually a lighter shovel for digging holes for plants, cultivating and edging.

B: D-handle shovels: This is the pointed one for scooping up sand, soil or gravel. You have to bend over a bit more with these because the length is shorter than the standard garden shovel.

C: **Long handle square point spade**. It is a bit heavier and can be used for edging or picking up grass, sand, gravel, or dirt that is against a wall or walkway barrier.

D: The **Transplanting spade** (same as a plumber's *sharpshooter)* is used for transplanting shrubs, plants or small trees that you put in the wrong spot the first time. The long narrow blade allows you to get *under* the roots and do less damage, and to dig a smaller, deeper hole.

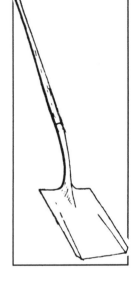

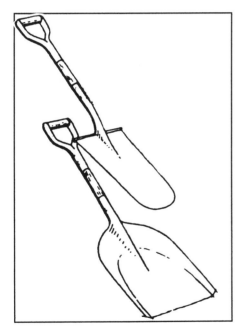

E: A **Scoop shovel** is used for picking up sawdust, fertilizer, manure, or gravel, anything you need to scoop.

HOES

The next item to buy is a *Hoe.* The standard garden hoe has a long solid wood handle (or fiberglass) with a 6 inch blade. Do the same in selecting this hoe as you do your shovel; lift it, swing it, see if it's balanced and get a good hoe with a strong steel blade.

The blade on most hoes will need to be sharpened periodically. Dirt will dull that hoe, same as it does a chain saw. Dirt has those fine particles of silicone and it takes the edge off that hoe blade in not too long a time. I'd say maybe a hoe needs resharpening several times during a gardening season. Matter of fact, there is no rule of thumb, when it gets dull, sharpen it.

Guess you have to make another stop in the hardware section and get a fairly nice sized *vise* and a file or two to sharpen this hoe, same as the point on your garden shovel. There are grinders for sale that cost as little a $25 or $30 that will do the job for you and make it easier to keep sharp. If you go into tools of any sort, this grinder is a useful tool.

A. This is the usual, everyday hoe with a blade width of 6 inches. It is relatively lightweight and does most of what you'll need.

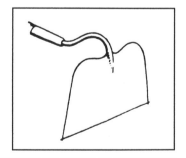

B. If you get serious about this gardening business, you might want to have a second hoe or maybe a third one. This hoe is called a *Warren hoe* and is used mainly for making furrows or cultivating between plants.

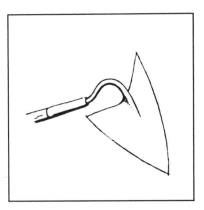

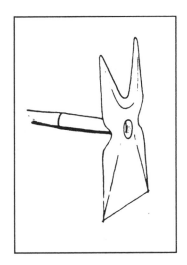

C. This *Weeding Hoe* is a two-parter; hoe on one side and a *gizmo* that helps pull out weeds on the other.

The best way I found to pull out weeds is with your hands. This brings us to another article you need, *gloves.* Again, try on several pair and buy one or two type and see which ones work best for you. Don't be afraid to pay from 3 to 5 dollars for a pair of good garden gloves. These are essential and you'll know what I mean if you try any extensive shoveling, raking or hoeing without them.

RAKES

Here are some drawings of rakes; the *Level Head rake* and the *Bow rake.* I don't think you need two of these general type right now. Go for the Bow rake. You can level soil, break up clumps of soil and handle it with greater ease. It is a sturdy, all-around utility rake.

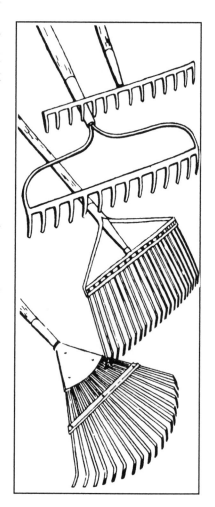

The other type of rake you should get right away is one of these used for raking grass and leaves. There are the *metal ones, bamboo type* and the *plastic* rakes.

Don't chinch on buying a rake either. It isn't that the most expensive rakes are the best, it's just that most of the time they are! An inexpensive rake will break, lose teeth and the handle will turn in your hands.

TROWELS

Another item you'll need right away is a *trowel*. These short-handled little shovels are for getting close to your plants. I prefer the standard trowel, the one with the sharper point and straight handle. Don't forget, get a good one. They are for sale in many stores for 99 cents or $1.49 but (again) get one that cost several bucks so the handle won't keep coming loose in your hand. Sharpen it too when it gets dull.

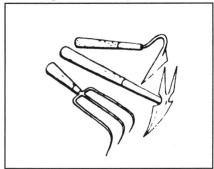 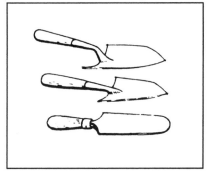

There are other items such as a small digger and a small hoe and perhaps even a hand weed puller. You know what I mean, you've seen these items that usually come in a set of three but if not, here's a drawing of them. You just choose *whatever* suits you, whatever makes it easier for you to do what you want to do in your garden.

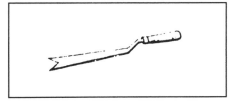

Remember to get some *knee pads* when you work in your garden or maybe one of those styrofoam sheets to kneel on. Your knees take an awful beating when they are unprotected and you're kneeling on grass or in soil.

And get yourself a pair of *coveralls* too, so that you can get them as dirty as you want then wash 'em out and hang them in your garage next to your gloves.

Not right now, if you have a new lawn and garden, but soon, when your garden begins to grow or if you have an existing garden, you'll need to add to your arsenal of tools such items as *Pruning Shears*, probably the most often used item in your garden after your shovel and rake.

Did I leave out a *garden hose?* I like a hose with a larger opening so I can get the water I want and adjust it from the nozzle. There are hoses that have 1/2, 5/8 and 3/4 inch openings and from 25 to 100 feet long.

This is when you have to get *a-measurin'* again because it depends on where you plan to use that hose. If you need an area watered that is say 85 feet away, you'll probably get a better buy on one, 100 foot hose as compared to two 50 foot hoses. If you need 140 feet, get a 100 and a 50 foot hose. There's no need to have *two* hundred feet of hose stacked high like you work for the fire department.

I'd get one hose for my front yard and one for my back yard because carrying those things around is not easy. Get a hanger of some type and they can be bought from 2 dollars for the one you can nail to wood or screw into the brick on the side of your house, up to about 40 dollars for the kind that you roll up and are on wheels.

Heck, you know most of that but some people don't think about it and I'd like to save you some time and money. I strongly recommend a quality hose that won't twist and kink up. It's just no fun going back to kick out a kink when you want water. If you have a camp or cabin in the woods, get the cheap hose because somebody will steal it.

Look for a good *Wheel Barrow* while you're at it. You'll need some help in getting those plants from your car or truck to where you want to plant them and for moving dirt and fertilizer from here to there. I prefer the mid-sized wheel barrow with the steel bed and a rubber, air-filled tire. They seem easier to push. But you look to see what is easiest for you to maneuver around.

There are some fine-looking, heavy duty *plastic* carts available of all shapes, sizes and strengths. I suggest, if expense is a consideration, that you go to a few stores and price them and look at the difference in quality of construction. Don't always go for price, remember? A sturdy cart, if taken care of properly, will outlast a half-dozen of the flimsy ones. Like a pitcher's legs, the wheels go out first.

Some of the last items to get if you want to become a successful gardener is a good broom, a dust pan, a couple of garbage cans, some strong garbage bags and a few of these new-fangled things somebody is always inventing that look like they'll make doing whatever it is you want to do easier.

SERIOUS, MORE EXPENSIVE GARDEN TOOLS

The first and largest item you'll need is a *Lawn mower.* A good self-propelled, *mulching* mower is my choice. If you have a large back yard, maybe you'll also want a riding mower that you can use on your front yard also. You'll still need, however, a smaller mower to get in close to things and to put on the finishing touches.

What a *mulching mower* does, is force the grass under it for a while so it can cut it several times thereby making smaller pieces to form this mulch that will decompose faster. For pine needles, get a bagger on whatever mower you have and use those pine needles for ground cover or mulch in your flower garden. And while you're at it, rake the pine cones before you cut or you'll be sharpening or replacing blades often.

Some lawn mower repair shops advise against a mulching mower. They say, by containing the grass the way it does, it tends to strain the engine. This could be true, so I'd recommend one with an engine larger than 3.75 horsepower to accommodate this extra burden in having to cut the grass several times.

I can't give you a whole bunch of information on the brand of lawn mower to buy, because it depends on your pocket book, the area you have to mow, the type of leaves that fall from your trees and your physical condition. All I can recommend is that you get a name brand mower with a satisfactory warranty. I saw a new mower made by *Ariens* you might look into. *Snapper* has always been a reliable mower. Look in *Consumer's Guide* to read what they say about the various brands. Their opinions are unbiased.

String Trimmers *(commonly known as Weed Eaters)* are excellent tools for getting around trees, along fences, helping you get weeds out of flower beds, edging sidewalks, trimming the grass in ditches or around culverts, and reaching spots that your lawn mower can't get to.

There's a new type of invention that some people put on their Weed Eater or String Trimmer that is made out of bicycle chain. Yet another is a cutting blade. Each look kinda dangerous to me.

But the editor of this book, who has a lawn that is over two acres, loves this chain. He disliked the string having to be replaced, untangled or unwound and says the chain lasts for months and cuts almost everything.

I've seen him get wild with it on the vines growing on his fenceline. He puts on a long sleeve shirt and goggles and gets a somewhat crazed look in his eyes then holds it up like an Uzi and fires away. It cuts everything and never needs restringing or unwinding. When the links wear down, he replaces them with links from a chain saw.

I cringe when I think of the damage it would do if it ever nicked his ankle when he has it on full throttle. There's no doubt it would cut right through bone. I have a friend we call *Three-toe Henry* who got whacked by one of these chains he put on his string trimmer. He can attest to the fact that they do not easily forgive negligience.

Even the string trimmers that still have the string can smart when the cord hits your leg or when a pebble or piece of stick is flung your way. When using one I insist you wear goggles, gloves and either high boots or the type of legends formerly worn by Boy Scouts or soldiers in World War I.

There are string trimmers that come in electric and gas, even ones that are battery powered. If you have a small yard and your extension cord can reach, why not select an electric trimmer? If you have a large front yard and/or a sizable back yard, or a lot of trees to wind around, I'd say get the gas type. If you have a large yard with light cutting, look at the battery powered model. Choose the one that will do what you need it to do.

An **Edger** is another useful tool although I've heard of some who edge with their string trimmers. I still use an edger because I like the neat, clean cut it makes. I have a lazy neighbor who puts two blades (sometimes three blades) on his edger so he can make only one pass to edge because he likes that wider cut.

I don't recommend that because the wider the valley, the more room there is for weeds to grow and the more chance you'll have for soil erosion. When it rains and the topsoil loosens, it could run down that "trench" and you'll be putting on new topsoil every year. Keep that thin, clean cut and use only one blade. If my neighbor buys this book, I'm in trouble.

You'll also need a **Spreader** for putting out seed or fertilizer. Some people spread with their hands but this is guess work. There are two basic types of spreaders; the *Broadcast* (left) and the *Drop* spreader (right). I like the broadcast type better because it seems to give even as well as thorough distribution.

There is also a hand-held spreader for smaller yards that works fine. It just doesn't hold as much seed or fertilizer as does the larger, walk-behind type.

Unless you have a very large front (and back) yard, I would not recommend purchasing a **Tiller**. If you need one, go rent it because it is more expensive to buy than most lawn mowers and you wouldn't use it nearly as often. I will go into more detail on why you should *buy* a tiller when I get my book out on vegetable gardening.

Chapter 3

YOUR LAWN

NEW YARDS

Ninety-nine percent of the new homes that are built, the builder installs the front yard. Most builders start with the grass first and they put in mostly *St. Augustine* grass. It works best, especially in these southern climates. As you go farther north past Dallas, they put in a type of rye grass because St. Augustine won't produce well in cold weather.

The thing to do is to talk to the builder *before* he puts the grass in because he will probably put in bank sand and smooth everything out nice and pretty to lay the grass on top. Woefully, some builders dump this bank sand over wood, brick, plaster, sheetrock and wire and cover that with bank sand then grass and you *think* you have a lawn whereas you have the semblance of a lawn over a garbage dump.

Now, I don't want to get in trouble with home builders over this statement but then, I don't care. The reputable builder would not do such a thing. Some builders, however, will. I've seen it more than once.

I suggest when you talk to your builder, have him clear your yard of the "big stuff" then go to your local nursery and ask them to come test your soil to see what nutrients you lack. Get your bank sand, the proper nutrients and till that soil maybe 5 or 6 inches deep. Then rake it flat, get out all remaining rock, stones, bricks, wood, etc., and now put in your grass. Do a thorough job now when it's easiest, because you'll never have that opportunity again.

If the soil is a gumbo or clay, till the bank sand into it and make it so it will drain. If you *really* care about this grass, call me during the program and I'll tell you what you need to know for a specific area or problem.

If you keep your lawn *well watered*, it will be healthy. I mean make it so wet for at least a month, that you won't want to walk on it for fear of sinking out of sight. You want your roots to establish because if your roots don't grow, you just have a bunch of dead grass laying on top of your soil.

SOIL PREPARATION

A vital part of planting anything is *soil preparation.* It's all part of planning your work, but is, in the opinion of many, a rather boring subject because there's so much to learn and most people want to plant when they want to plant. Let me make it as simple as I can for you.

Everything that grows, grows in soil. Very few soils have the natural ingredients it takes to grow things the way man likes them to grow; fast, pure, beautiful, and trouble free. Soil is an element made up of a mixture of water, sand, clay, silt, organic matter and living organisms. And, there are various types of soil but we don't have the time or space to go into all of this. All you need be concerned with for now, is the type of soil in your yard.

It takes time for soil to form, as well as climate, parent material, living organisms and topography. Soil can be good or poor, heavy or light, fine or coarse, sandy loam or clay and before you plant anything, it's wise to find out what kind of soil you have so you can do something about it.

Oh, I know. Some of you have fathers or grand fathers who never paid much attention to any of this, yet they grew fine crops year after year. Trust me, friends and neighbors, for every one who grew great flowers or excellent food crops, there were dozens more we never hear about who failed miserably.

Take full advantage of modern technology and the extensive research put into finding out all about soil that produces great whatever-it-is you want to grow. To do this, make that trek back to your local nursery and ask them to analyze your soil. I'd recommend *they* do it the first time and you watch.

It's possible for you to do this on your own. You can purchase a soil test kit from almost any lawn and garden center or nursery and just follow the instructions. Then, listen to my program and find out what you can do to whatever type of soil you have.

There's a company in Hondo, Texas by the name of *Medina Agriculture Products* who seem to have all the answers as far as ways to condition your soil regardless of it's makeup. Give them a call at **(210) 426-3011** for their product and price brochure. It will be well-worth the effort.

A product we've been pushing on GardenLine is *Soil Pro.* They advertise with KTRH sure, but even if they didn't, the results I've seen with their Soil Pro 200, 400 and 600 has been so outstanding that I'd recommend them anyway. You can call them at **(713) 893-8088 or 1-800-829-0215.**

A healthy plant, like a healthy body with proper nutrients, *resists* disease. Yes, man has been the only one able to change and modify soil conditions almost instantly to provide suitable soil with which to grow things. Take advantage of what we've learned and do it right.

In Houston alone, there are over 45 soil types with three basic configurations being sand, clay and loam. In fertilizers, you need the correct combination of nitrogen, phosphorous and potassium for your particular soil to have "good" soil for planting.

I know that many of you are just trying your hand at this for the first time and I'd lose the lot of you if I went into any more detail that I'm doing now. That's why, to keep things simple for soil preparation, I recommend you get all the information you can on *Soil Pro* and on these *Medina* products. The best informaiton I can share with you now is the difference between dirt and soil. Soil is what you use for planting. Dirt is what you get under your fingernails.

Remember, call **KTRH** when *GardenLine* is on because we get reports all the time on new products and the successes people have gotten with the products I mention throughout this book.

CHOOSING GRASS

My favorite is *St. Augustine.* You'll see it on most of the lawns in ouston.   It requires medium maintenance and just needs to be cut every 7 or so days and enjoys a good watering maybe once a week. It can get by with partial sun but likes full sun. It is a medium green in color and can be mowed every week to ten days.

Bermuda grass comes in two basic types; *Common Bermuda* and *Bermuda hybrids.* The Common Bermuda grass needs full sun. You can plant from seed in late spring when the soil temperature warms up to 70 degrees.

The *Hybrid Bermuda* also needs full sun, is a darker green in color and it should also be planted in late spring. It requires a high degree of maintenance and needs cutting maybe twice a week during the growing season which is all year long except in the colder months. Bermuda grass might turn brown in winter but greens up again in spring.

The *maintenance* on Bermuda grass is different than St. Augustine in that it needs a *reel-type* lawn mower for cutting, you know, the kind you used to hate to push when you were a youngster in the 40' and 50's. Available now, are the reel-type with *motors* on them. Still, more of a specialty mower.

Rye is the grass for winter and is a very bright green. It's beautiful on lawns and you can throw seeds down in maybe September or October and it should show itself until as late as mid-March, again, depending on the climate. Rye is more commonly known as *winter grass* because . . . it grows in winter!

TIP: When buying grass, find out if it's been fertilized. If it has, wait until a later date to fertilize again so you won't burn the grass.

PLANTING GRASS

PLUGS - SEEDS - SPRIGS - SOD - STOLONS

Most of the grass you'll buy from a nursery come on pallets with grass cut into 12 x 15 inch blocks. *Plugs* are small sections of sod that you can cut from these blocks in 4 inch square sections and placed about a foot apart. This is an inexpensive way of putting in grass because you can stretch 1 square yard of solid sod to maybe 20 to 30 square yards of grass that should fill in the empty spaces in 4 to 5 months. Not a bad way to go.

Some books I've read recommend that you cut off and plant plugs in 2 inch squares but I don't like taking my chances with this size. A 2 inch square might wash away and the roots have a tendency to dry out more easily. You'll save money and get adequate coverage from the 4 inch squares and your success rate will more than double.

Seeds are the slow way to go. The only way I recommend seeding is if you have acres of soil to plant and/or lots of time to wait until something grows. This is, of course, the least expensive way.

Sprigs are not my choice simply because it takes time and bending over to plant them. My experience with sprigs (pieces of stem torn from sod, hopefully with roots and leaves) is that they dry out and you are left with clumps of dead grass on bare soil. They could be blown away in a wind or washed away in a hard rain and you need to plant each and every one.

Sod is my first choice simply because when it's done, it's done and only maintenance is necessary. Make certain the edges meet to cover the area completely and then roll it. You can rent a roller from most rent-all companies for maybe $15 or so dollars for a day. It's light enough to load in the trunk of your (big) car to get it home. Then, fill it with water, roll it over your grass to even it and then empty the tank and return the roller. Then, of course, deep-water that grass.

Putting out *Stolons* gets the same recommendation from me as seeding for a front yard; I don't like it. To stolonize, you simply scatter sprigs over the soil and water it, maybe spread some top soil over it and water it more, hoping the grass will grow.

Matter of fact, I don't even know why I mentioned it other than to impress you with a few words you will run across if there is some gardening in your life. Stick with the sod or the 4 inch plugs and you'll be safe.

TIP: When you plan to have a house built, most mortgage companies automatically loan on a front yard only. This means that you have to add a few thousand dollars (or more) for the back yard. Ask the builder to tack it on to the price so you can put it on your mortgage. It might raise your payments a few dollars a month but it is certainly worth it and far better than having to come up with several thousand dollars cash to add on to the money you already paid out.

ESTABLISHED LAWNS

Grass needs nourishment, and gets its nourishment through water and fertilizer. The ideal times to *feed* your grass is **April 1st** (April Fool's day), **July 4th** (Independence Day), and **October 1st** (first day after the end of September). To insure this grass will grow the best it can, I prefer the *Easy Gro Premium* a **19-5-9 NPK**. Researchers from Texas A&M University say St. Augustine grass prefers a **3-1-2, 15-5-10, 19-5-9,** It will be marked in large numbers on the bag.

You can put this fertilizer out in liquid or granule form. The liquid can be done by buying one of those hand-held sprayers that fit on the end of your garden hose. Instructions are on the fertilizer container as to how much to use for what. The sprayer comes with simple instructions. All you need to do is read the dial and set it on the correct amount. It's really quite easy.

For the granule fertilizer, the *Broadcast spreader* throws the fertilizer granules out in a sorta' cyclone effect and covers the ground well. I like it best because it misses very little and spreads evenly. It too has a dial where you can adjust the amount you want dispensed.

With a *Drop spreader*, if you miss a spot you'll know it when the grass grows and has a dark green spot and a light green spot, a dark green spot and a . . . well, you get the idea. You can see what I mean when you use a riding mower and make turns.

More often than not you'll leave a "Mohawk-type" slash of grass that you have to go back over, right? But, you can't see your error while fertilizing until the grass grows, healthy where the fertilizer landed and, well, less than healthy in the other spots.

PROBLEMS IN USING A DROP SPREADER

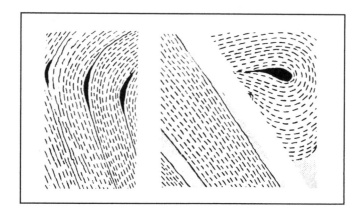

If you already have a drop spreader, I suggest using the *checkerboard* pattern, go up and down your yard then across your yard and use half strength fertilizer; twice the work but it gets the job done.

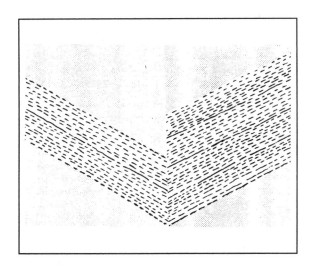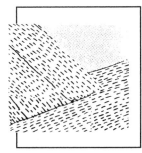

WAYS TO FERTILIZE WITH A DROP SPREADER

After you mow your grass and fertilize your grass, water your grass. Water infrequently but thoroughly. If you let your water run all night, your grass will suffer. That's too much. Your grass may not die but it might have a purple tinge to it.

TIP: If you want green lawns in winter, sprinkle *rye grass* seed amongst your St. Augustine. Don't worry about injuring the St. Augustine, it is still there and will grow again in spring.

As far as the height to cut your grass, this is a personal thing. Too low is when the sun hits it and turns the leaves a light brown. Too high is when you throw a softball in it and you can't see it unless you step on it. I think 2 to 2 1/2 inches tall is ideal. The reason is that the more foliage you have on your St. Augustine, the more shade you have on the soil and less evaporation on these hot summer days.

One thing to remember about the type of grass you choose is the type of tree you choose. Some grasses need full sun and some only partial sun. In the entire Houston area, there is not a grass to date that will grow in dense shade.

FERTILIZING YOUR LAWN

There are three major elements in fertilizer - *nitrogen, phosphorous* and *potassium.* When you look at a package or sack of fertilizer, there are large numbers that read **10-5-15** (for instance) and this simply means that it contains 10 parts nitrogen, 5 parts phosphorous and 15 parts potassium. If the numbers read **10-10-10** you know there are equal parts of the three elements.

The **NPK** you might see on some bags of fertilizer stand for nitrogen, phosphorus and potassium. The "K" kind of throws you but that's simply the chemical symbol for potassium that was also known as *kalium.* You also might hear some people talk of *potash* instead of potassium. Potash is the *oxide* in potassium, potassium hydroxide. It's chemical symbol is K_2O. Now that's kinda interesting, isn't it?

Let's take it slow now and go over what these various elements represent.

a. Nitrogen - an element in your soil that gives your grass a greener, healthier color and increases the growth of the stem and foliage.

b. Phosphorous - an element used to stimulate all phases of plant growth. It hardens plants for cold weather, promotes greater seed and flower formation as well as root growth.

c. Potassium - helps plants resist disease and damage from cold and insects. Plants use potassium to maintain their salt balance. Potassium also promotes production of sugar, starches, and oil for food.

For fertilizing your lawn, I have to yield to the **3-1-2** ratio of elements year round. Some of the experienced lawn companies go with a **2-1-1** ratio in spring and in the fall, a **1-2-2** count to encourage healthy root growth before a freeze. Other than this, your lawn need nothing additional. To be safe, I'd go with the recommendation from researchers at Texas A&M and stick with the **3-1-2 NPK** rating.

There is a **13-13-13** general type fertilizer that you get away with using just about anywhere, and a **12-24-12** for your garden area. This feeds vegetables but there are many specialty vegetable fertilizers on the market. In the fall of the year, about October, you use *Easy Gro Winterize* on your grass. You won't see any healthy green grass on top but the roots will grow. A good, healthy root system will make great grass in spring.

Chapter 4

TREES

CHOOSING A TREE

The very first growing thing I'd plant in my new front yard would be a tree. You should build "around" a tree in that it will be the predominant growing thing in your yard. Besides, if you chose a big tree, why track all over your newly sodded, wet grass? Remember, I said water it a lot? I advise you to plant your tree before you plant your grass.

Make certain you know everything there is to know about this tree. Read what I have to say about it, do some extensive reading solely about that particular tree, then follow that up by asking a gardener or nurseryman whose judgement and knowledge you trust.

Some people want their grass in before they pick a tree. That's okay too, if your grass has been down, watered in and dry for at least 15 days. Just be careful of the damage you might do to your lawn if the tree is too big. I say first, trees, then hedge, shrubs, grass and plants in that order.

Before we get into specific trees, let me tell you about *deciduous (dee-sid-you-us)* trees, ones that lose their leaves in the fall. To confuse you a bit more, there are these deciduous trees that although they lose their leaves, their trunk and branches take on a fine, fall color and they look great all year round, leaves or not. Others in wintertime look like dead sticks. I'll tell about each as we move along.

The other general type of tree is the *evergreen* tree that is just that, it is *ever* green, it does not lose its leaves in winter. Sometimes, when explaining to you about a certain tree, I'll mark it with a big (**D**) or (**E**) and sometimes I'll just tell you if it keeps or loses its leaves, okay?

Most everybody wants the fast growing, inexpensive shade tree, something that will grow quick and be easy to care for. We all want something that is cheap and good. It reminds me of a story about a used car salesman.

A fella' walked up to him and said, *"I'd like to have a good, cheap used car."* The salesman looked at him and smiled. *"Make up your mind, do you want a **good** one or do you want a **cheap** one?"* The two words rarely go together. Same as with trees, matter of fact, same with everything!

A good thing to do is to look through your neighborhood and see what kind of trees your neighbors have. Pick out the kind that suits you then go to a nearby nursery to price them.

In choosing the *size* of trees, I recommend you spend a little extra money and buy a larger tree. The bigger tree you set in your yard, the healthier the root system and the faster it will become established. I'd get a tree that was in a 50 gallon, preferably a 100 gallon pot. The larger one might cost 150 to 250 dollars more but that tree will be there for as long as you live in that house, probably for as long as you live. It's only a *one time* investment.

While we're on the subject of trees, I do not like trees planted in clusters, no matter who says what. Let me tell you why. They are difficult to mow around, their roots entangle, if one tree gets a disease the other gets it too, you'll have a problem in which branches to trim and the tree is, in essence, twice as thick and little sunlight, if any, can seep through.

Now, let me tell you about the hazards of tree *roots* and this is why it's smart to draw that sketch so you'll be able to prevent what will eventually happen with these roots.

TREE ROOTS IN YOUR YARD

Most of the "good" trees that you plant in your yard will be there forever, and as this tree grows, so grows the root. In fact, it's hard to believe that the part *under* ground, the roots on some trees, are oftentimes almost as large as the part you see *above* ground. But it is!

That's why it's smart to choose the type of tree that is conducive to the surroundings as well as to measure the distance that tree (even large shrubs) is to be from your walkway, driveway and most certainly, your house.

Some people say, *"Plant the big trees in your back yard where there's room. Big trees will certainly damage the foundation of your house in your front yard somewhere along the way."* This is not necessarily true.

What the tree does, is their feeder roots, the little tiny hair roots, the ones you can barely see, are the ones that are doing the job and eating and drinking for the tree itself. They will grow up to the foundation line and pull moisture *out* from under your house. When they do this, it creates a dry spot, probably a hole, and the weight of your house falls a bit and your foundation will crack.

To prevent this, you construct a *root barrier.* One of the pioneers of this is *Foster's Tree Service* in Houston. Their telephone number is **(713) 458-5992.** If you forget the number, just dial **F-O-S-T-E-R-S.** Neat, huh?

What they do is dig a trench around your house and put in the barrier material, which is a plastic sheet, not unlike the plastic many put on the walls of their greenhouses or patio roofs. This trench needs to be only about 18 inches deep, and it stops these feeder roots from penetrating the area at or under your structure.

Again, maybe for the third time in as many chapters, in the words or Ross Perot, *"Measure twice and cut once."* It is always smart to plan before you do any cutting or planting. If you're in a new subdivision and are building a house and have little to go by as example, go to a subdivision nearest you and see what they have. Be smart about spending a lot of money and do it right the first time.

A rule of thumb is that the tree should not drape over your house. Since the root system is about as large (or larger) than the tree branches, if you plant a tree that has a 50 foot *tree branch spread* you should plant it 35 feet from your house, at least. You don't want leaves on your roof because if you don't sweep or rake them of, moisture gathers in them and you have a sort of mulch on your roof. If left unattended, it will cause leaks.

I don't think it's necessary to be too concerned over tree roots near your walkway. Oh, I would not ever plant right *next* to one but your walkway usually has only about 4 inches of cement and chances are you'll be able to see the tree roots as they approach and "cut them off at the pass."

The feeder roots will go underneath but if you see a larger root creeping too close to your sidewalk or driveway, I'd just take a *sharpshooter* and cut the end off that anchor root that wants to lift up that concrete. You won't hurt the tree, only change the direction of the roots.

The *drip line* is at the edge of your tree. In other words, the outer edge of your tree where the water falls off, like the edge of an umbrella, is your drip line. So when we speak of watering and feeding at the drip line, it's not at the trunk where the water runs down, but at the outer edge of your tree.

Now, let's say you're a little short on cash or want the adventure and experience of digging a tree from the wilderness to take home and plant, "the littl'er the tree the better." The main reason is that you'll get more of the root system in a smaller tree and it will be undamaged or have less damage.

I've known of many people who wanted to bring home a 6 or 7 foot pine tree from their hunting or fishing cabin in the Piney Woods. They make two errors, one is that the soil conditions are not similar, and with a tree that large, unless they dig very deep, they cut a lot of roots. Many end up with a pine *telephone pole* in their yard that never grows.

MY FAVORITE TREES

Green Ash is a terrific tree, as is the **White Ash...NOT** the **Arizona Ash** (brittle, prone to disease and insect damage, and has a life-span of as little as 5 and as long as 12 years).

The **Green Ash** grows to as high as 80 feet with about a 40 foot umbrella. It can grow in sun or semi-shade in moist, organic soil. It is a medium-fast growth tree and excellent for shade. It drops it's leaves in winter but keeps a yellow to purple hue and is a really fine tree. As is the ... **White Ash** that's a mite shorter (maybe 5 or so feet) with the same wing span but with a more oval leaf. This tree is all over the south and is native to Louisiana, Georgia and Texas. It has a long life span, by long I mean 50, 75 years or more.

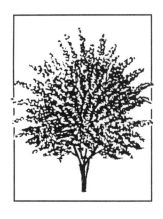

Crape Myrtle . . . you'll see them in many front yards because they are relatively small trees. They grow to about 20 feet high with a branch diameter of 15 feet. They need 5 or 6 hours of sun each day and bloom well in summer as well as early fall. When you choose a tree, to be certain of its color, choose when it is bloom, maybe 6 to 8 feet high. You can select from red, white, lilac or pink flowers.

There are a variety of Crape Myrtle *hybrids* that grow as high as 30 feet. The *Japanese Crape Myrtle* has a branch span almost as tall as it is but it can be pruned back and shaped. These can also be used as large shrubs if you cut them back yearly.

American Holly . . . this is a beautiful tree that stays green all year long. It grows to about 30 feet tall and spreads out maybe 20 feet. It likes sun but can tolerate some shade. The growth is rather slow but the tree seems to live forever. For those beautiful red berries that grow during the cold season, you have to get at least two trees, one male and one female. The female is the one that is most beautiful, unlike tropical fish. But remember, like most women, it needs a man around to make it really lovely and bear those red berries.

Burford Holly . . . almost a large bush but labeled a tree nevertheless. It grows to about ten feet in height and spreads out maybe 6 or 8 feet. It too stays green year round and likes full sun. The Holly family are all evergreens. Look at several types to see which suits you. They help keep your yard from looking bare in winter.

* A fairly new tree to this area is called **Luster Leaf Holly** that grows to about 25 feet with branches maybe 15 to 18 feet. The branches are silver-gray in color and the leaves are glossy green with an aromatic fragrance. Remember, buy two and get them married if you want those red berries.

Ligustrum . . . yep, it's a tree! It grows to a height of 20 feet with a 10 foot umbrella. It can grow in full sun or part shade, and tolerates most soil and needs little maintenance. You can shape them as you choose and cut off the lower branches to make a trim nice tree that sports green leaves all year long. Chances are, it'll last longer than you.

Southern Magnolia . . . grows only to about 60 feet with a spread of 35 feet. It grows in full or partial sun and needs fertilizer with a high nitrogen content. It stays green all year and has the most wonderful fragrance and blooms large, 6 inch in diameter, cream colored flowers. It's dense foliage almost kills whatever it under it but it can be trimmed to allow sun to seep through.

There are *cultivars* (family members of the Magnolia) that are smaller such as *Russet Beauty* and *Little Gem* that grow to a height of 25 feet with a span of about 10 feet.

Drummond Red Maple . . .. is a beautiful tree that is deciduous *(no leaves in winter)* and is fast-growing and gets to a height of 65 feet with a spread of about 35 feet. It is a colorful tree with small red flowers in sppring, red leaf stems in summer and has a red or yellow foliage in fall.

A Mimosa
is a beautiful tree that loses its leaves in winter and grows as wide as it does high, maybe to 30 feet. It likes sun and will tolerate almost any soil. It's blooms are puffs of pink or yellow pink in May and June and attracts hummingbirds. It is a fast-growth tree that gives quick shade with fern-like foliage and an umbrella shape. It is, however, short-lived. It might last 15 or so years.

Live Oak . . . my favorite tree along with the Drummond Red Maple and the Shumard Oak. It grows maybe as high as 50 feet with a wing spread of 75 feet. It tolerates most soil conditions and likes full sun. It has the strongest of wood and is resistant to breakage, insects or diseases and lives for years and years; a few lifetimes, at least.

The Live Oak is a majestic tree but will take up a lot of space. You'll need a sizable front yard so it won't overwhelm everything else. But if you have room, like maybe a large front yard, big back yard or along a drive (like Oak Alley in Louisiana) it is wondrous. It is an evergreen and will withstand cruel winters and hot summers. If you cut the branches to shape it, spray or brush that special tree paint on the wounds.

Shumard Oak . . . a wonderful tree for Texas, especially Houston. It grows to 60 feet with a 40 foot shade umbrella. It likes full sun, moist soil and is tolerant as far as neglect and disease. It has a reddish-bronze foliage in fall and is green in the summertime. Pick one out in fall to make certain you get one with a bright red color to it. It is really and truly a beautiful tree. They are, what I would call, "kid friendly." Both oaks are excellent for building a tree house for your kids. They endure nailed-in boards and nailed-on flooring for tree houses and have large, firm limbs to hug on to.

Pecan . . . everybody likes to eat pecans, and pecan trees are favorites when you have lots of room. I have a friend who has a huge pecan tree in her front yard and she distributes those thin-shelled beauties throughout the neighborhood. The pecan tree is mildly dense and allows sun to seep through so grass growth is there. Call *Paul's Precious Pecans* at **1-800-352-4061** for pecan news and information.

Pecan trees like sun, fertile, deep, moist soil. They do, however, take a degree of maintenance, especially spraying against pests. They live forever and some grow to a height of 80 feet with a 65 foot spread.

There are many varieties and some bear such small pecans they shouldn't be labeled fruit trees. For the biggest and best pecans, look for the trees that have Indian names such as Choctaw, Pawnee or Cheyenne. The Stewart and Mayhan trees have tasty fruit but the nuts are small.

Pine . . . not my favorite tree for front yards or around my house because of the droppage of needles and pine cones, but wonderful trees for farms and ranches and in large back yards. The *Loblolly pine,* an evergreen, grows to a height of 80 feet or more with a span of maybe 35 feet. The other types, the *Longleaf pine* and *Shortleaf pine* run rampant in East Texas and are easy to grow in almost any soil.

Chinese Tallow . . . this tree is everywhere in and around Houston and just grows and grows. I have four and I cut them down yearly but the next year, they are up again. Actually, it's a trouble-free tree and has a nicce blend of red, yellow, orange, even purplish fall color.

It grows fast and seems to never die. You can probably ask anyone who has a vacant lot in or around Houston if they'll give you one and chances are they will. Get one maybe 4 to 6 feet tall and shape it as it grows. Some form five or six trunks and they cluster and stay green almost all year long.

Willow . . . there's the *Corkscrew* and the *Weeping Willow* from which to choose, as well as a half-dozen other varieties pl won't mention. The Corkscrew Willow grows in sun or some shade, in any soil, but likes water. Some actually root in water. The branches are spirally and twisting (interesting, I think) with narrow leaves that stay green all year long.

The Weeping Willow likes full sun, any soil and likes it best in or near water. The branches actually sag...they *weep*. They have shallow roots that invade sewer lines, drawn to them because of their need for water. Prune and trim to desired shape. Excellent for around ponds and for the shore of your fishing cabin.

Yaupon . . . a really nice tree for your front yard. It grows to maybe 20 feet high with a 12 to 15 foot wing spread and is tolerant of most soil and likes shade or sun. It is a medium-growth tree and provides little shade. The female tree (again) has the red berries so buy one in winter when the berries are exposed to determine the sex of the tree.

I don't think a male counterpart is needed for these berries to show up, and the tree can endure almost any conditions. In early spring, trim *inside* branches to keep outer shape uniform. If you prune *outside* branches, next season berries will not appear whether you get a male tree or not to coax the growth.

The **Gingko** tree grows to a height of 30 feet with a 20 foot spread. It likes sun and any soil that has good drainage. The foliage is fern-like and fan-shaped. It's a hardy tree that is drought resistant, tolerates environmental stress and resists insects and diseases. Buy only the male Gingko tree because the female bears fruit and emits a foul odor.

If you notice a lesser price in a Gingko tree, chances are it's a female tree. The Gingko is yellow in fall, is deciduous, but the branches in winter take on an autumn-gold color. A beautiful tree.

A **Tulip tree** grows to 60 feet with a spread of about 20 feet and is sometimes called a **Yellow Poplar.** It prefers sun and rich, deep, well-drained soil. When it blooms in spring, its tulip-shaped flowers are green, yellowish and with a fall color of bright yellow. It loses its leaves in winter, but is an excellent summertime shade tree with deep roots. It also attracts hummingbirds.

TIP: A fact to remember about a tree is that the height shouldn't frighten you. If you choose a tree that is marked as reaching 60 or 70 or 80 feet, it takes a lot of time for this to happen. Many people move in an out of a house in 8 to 10 years.

It isn't like the "old days" when a family passed the house on for generations. For a tree to reach maturity and get to the height that most books have them marked, it might take 30 to 50 years.

To be safe, find a tree that you like and if it looks like you're going to live in that house forever, make certain you have plenty of room in your front yard or put the thing in your back yard. If you take these prevent-measures of digging a small ditch around your house for a root barrier, if you water the tree and let the roots go deep and/or cut the roots that invade the top, you'll be okay.

When cutting these tree roots that are exposed, make certain you cut only a few, you know, one on this side and one on the other. Chances are they won't all be sticking up but if so and you cut too much, you could kill that tree.

REMOVING A TREE STUMP

Let me share with you some experience I've had with removing a tree stump. **Don't do it yourself!** Call up a stump removing company because it will be done right and will probably be less expensive. Dial **F-O-S-T-E-R-S.**

Cutting the tree down is no real problem because you probably enjoy hacking away with your chain saw; most men do. Just be careful not to let that tree fall on your house, garage or fence, or worse yet, your neighbors house!

After thinking about it a minute, I think you had better leave the stump-removal and cutting that tree down to the professionals. One fall from that tree and the doctor bill for a broken arm or leg is much higher than the cost the tree company will charge for doing the work. Call Foster Tree Service for an estimate. It would be a wise move.

Removing the stump is not a bit of fun, let me tell you. You will have to dig and dig with that shovel, chop away with that ax or dull your chain saw every time you cut into the mud and actually never get to the entire root. Or, you'll have to get a trailer hooked on your car or truck and go rent a *stump grinder* and the rent on it alone will probably be more than the stump removal company would charge.

I see different chemicals advertised in magazines they say will *rot* that root or trunk but I've never had good luck with those and it takes months and months to work. No sir (or ma'am), I suggest you earn your living the way you know how and get the ones who earn theirs removing tree stumps to do that other job for you. It always pays in the long run, I promise you.

Chapter 5

PLANTS AND SHRUBS

LOCATION

We have touched on grass and trees, now let's get to putting the finishing touches on that schematic. I know I told you to "plan your work and to work your plan" and I still want you to do that but really, when it all comes down to it, a yard rarely, if ever, looks the way you want it from the way it is drawn on paper.

What most people end up doing is, after they put it down on paper to get the measurements and to see *about* what they are doing, they buy the plants and shrubs and put them out in containers on the spots they have marked.

Then they move them around like chess pieces, back up, look at them, ask their spouse what they think, get an opinion orrtwo from a friend or neighbor, sleep on it and move them around again the next day - and maybe the next.

Some even plant them then dig them up again, so I advise to just dig the holes and *set* the plants gingerly in

Some even plant them then dig them up again, so I advise to just dig the holes and *set* the plants gingerly in them. When it *seems* that what you have set out pleases you, push the dirt in around them.

TIP: If you have a large Oak or Red Maple tree in your yard and you want to add some plants and shrubs. If you plan to build *around* that tree, what you don't want to do is build *up* around it.

If you do, get an aluminum or plastic collar to wrap around the trunk where the trunk meets the dirt. I'd advise putting in maybe only 2 inches of soil per season. You see, the tree roots are alive and they burn oxygen. If you cut off this oxygen supply by smothering the roots with dirt, the tree will suffer, perhaps even die.

SHRUBS

For shrubs near the house, a rule of thumb is, never plant them too close. Ideally, you should have room to walk between these shrubs and your house. Give that shrub some room to grow and give whoever is going to tend to them room to work.

The types of shrub I see most often in the Houston area and is most parts of Texas are *Wax Leaf Ligustrum, Red Tipped Photinia, Boxwood, and Pitosporum,* all excellent choices and lovely, durable plants.

The *Red Tipped Photinia* (**fo-tin-e-ah**) is the one I love most; it grows quickly, it's relatively inexpensive, and it endures almost any weather and neglect. It grows as high as 12 feet (in case you need privacy or hate your next-door neighbors) and likes sun. New leaves are a bronzy-red with the bottoms a deep green all year long. They are easy to trim and take up as much as 4 feet when at full growth. You can shape them into a small tree but they make a terrific *living fence* for around hot tubs, fences or along a walkway.

These shrubs can grow high but that's why God invented pruners *(did God really invent these clippers?)* so you can cut the shrubs the height you want them, somewhere between two and three feet. If you want to *block* a view or hide your neighbor's unkempt garage or sad front yard from view, let these shrubs grow high. They are gorgeous.

The *Wax Leaf Ligustrum* (**lig-gust-trum**) is almost in the same category as is it's neighbor above, the Red Tipped Photinia. It is hardy, takes neglect with somewhat of a smile, grows as high as 9 feet and is green year round.

It sports quarter-inch white flowers in small clusters in early summer followed by black berries in the fall. Birds like these berries too so you can have a fast-growing, hardy hedge that is also a kindly bird brunch-stop.

You really have a wide choice in this family, from a tree-sized shrub *(California Privet)* that grows to 20 feet tall with dark green waxy-type leaves, to a *Curly Ligustrum* that grows to about 8 feet tall, or a *Golden Ligustrum* that is about 4 by 4, and a *Ligustrum tree* that is 25 feet high and about 15 feet across, to the *Japanese* or *Wax Leaf Ligustrum* that tops about 12 feet high with a 7 foot spread.

TIP: The California Privet is lovely and looks great in a garden but they seem to be "manufacturing plants" for White Fly. Ask your nurseryman about that to double-check me on this. I'm sure this is accurate.

All of these Ligustrum family members are lovely, evergreen and can be shaped. They like sun or part shade, some water, are disease resistant, hardy, and can be trimmed or pruned as you like. In winter they have blue berries on orange stems and have variegated cultivars.

You've seen many of the wax leaf form trimmed into three or four round balls *(Poodle Trees)* as decorator shrubs at entry ways. They can be found at almost any garden center and are three to four dollars for a one-gallon can. They grow quickly and the balls are fun and easily shpaed.

You see a lot of *Boxwood* as a shrub or hedge, mostly along walkways. The main reason is that Boxwood too is easy to grow, easy to maintain and stays green year round. Before you make your mind up on these shrubs I mention, go to your lawn and garden store and *look* at different shrubs. Ask the nurseryman what is best for your particular area and they will show you the plant itself and you decide then.

Pittosporum, **(pit-ah-spore-um)** yet another popular, inexpensive, easy-to-grow and maintain shrub. Can take full sun or lots of shade and won't hurt when you prune it to shape it the way you like. It is an evergreen and can grow to 20 feet in height with a spread of more than half that.

In the South; in Alvin, Angleton, Lake Jackson, Texas City, Clear Lake, Galveston where it doesn't get that cold, the plant will do well. Where it gets cold, North Houston up to and through Dallas, it has to be protected.

There are several varieties of Pitosporum from which you might choose, some with dark green to a greenish-gray leaves as well as the *variegated (having diverse colors in streaks or splotches)* type that have whitish tips on the ends of the leaves.

Cleyera (Cleyera japonica) is a great shrub that doesn't ever bloom but has a beautiful, lush, green color to it year round. It needs to be planted on the south side of the house in the shade. Visit an arboretum and see what's in there. These shrubs are all marked with information on each.

The people who work these places are actually tickled to death to have you ask a question and they will impress you with their answers. I enjoy visiting these places and I ask them for information too. I learn new things daily.

Pampas grass likes full sun, any soil that does not retain water and is drought tolerant. I usually cut mine back in winter for a full spring growth. They grow into large clumps and take up a lot of space, like as much as 10 by 10 feet high and wide with light green leaves that are narrow, 6 to 8 feet long, and sharp-edged. Never pull on them with ungloved hands. They'll cut like a razor.

Pampas grass makes a stalwart fence if you plant it 3 or 4 feet apart. If not watered in winter, they turn brown but still block entry. Although *drought tolerant*, I've found that the more you water it, the better and greener it will grow.

Some Pampas grass has large stalks that grow above this "clump" with whisker-like ends the size of a football.
You can get it in 1 or 5 gallon pots at your nursery but remember, the leaves are sharp, so be careful while handling it. Looks beautiful when it shows it's white flower, and doesn't look too bad in the winter either.

Nandina, a popular shrub with red berries and a reddish foliage that will grow in shade in almost any soil. In cold winters, prune ground branches and shape the bush. It grows to a height of 6 feet and can be a small or a large shrub depending on how you shape it. It grows out to maybe a diameter of 3 feet.

Oleander is another popular evergreen shrub with flowers that range in color from white through red and yellow through orange and needs full sun to bloom but careful with them around small children. Books say that all parts are poisonous if eaten!

that the plant has an extremely bitter taste and does, in fact, has poisonous as well as medicinal properties.

As a kid living in the country, I remember putting all sorts of grass and weeds in my mouth. I even tried Oleander and spit it out quickly. I think, to be fatal, a person would have to be fed a lot of leaves and branches. The records show that for those few who actually ingested Oleander for some unknown reason, that nausea and vomiting usually occur and most of the toxin is vomited up.

They're beautiful, just don't eat 'em. I might even call an Oleander almost a tree because varieties of Oleander grow to as high as 10 feet with an 8 foot spread to as low as 4 feet with a 3 foot spread. To make them even more hardy than they already are, almost stop watering them in August. They are drought tolerant.

Sago Palms are attractive. Don't plant them too close to the sidewalk or where you'll be walking because the palms will play havoc with stockings or silk trousers, even legs. They come up with little pups, and when you see some pups growing, you can get your shovel, dig down and separate the pup from its mother.

If you can, try to get some roots with the dislodged pup and reset it in a container or in another part of the yard and you'll have another sago palm. I think they look prettier when their pups are removed. I'd get me some *Medina Plus* and soak the roots in water for 12 hours, then replant them.

The *Yaupon Holly* (pronounced **yo-pon** by most...but "some say to-may-toes and some say ta-maat-oes. Some say po-tay-toes and some say pa-taat-toes...etc") has small, dark green leaves with red berries. While pruning, cut inside branches to keep its natural shape. Again, the "lady" tree is the one with the berries.

Dwarf Yaupon grows in full sun or part shade and is a hardy plant, oftentimes used as walkway shrubs the same as Boxwood. It is green and dense and will tolerate most soils but likes to drink once in a while and enjoys garden soil. If you fertilize it in late winter with a balanced fertilizer it makes a healthier, bushier plant.

Yucca - Yuk-a is right! The *Spanish* yucca is also called a *Bayonet* yucca for obvious reasons. They have upright, pointed, sharp, stiff leaves that are dangerous to children, pets and adults. I **do not recommend** this plant unless you are building a perimeter of defense around your home.

There is the *Red Yucca* however, that is not as sharp-pointed and is a coral-pink in color and is popular in many rock gardens since it likes sun and sandy loam soil. Then, there is the *Soft Leaf Yucca* that enjoys much the same conditions as the others (sun, sandy loam soil) doesn't need much water and can grow almost anywhere there is sun and sand and the leaves are shrubby and soft, dagger-shaped but harmless and with the same beauty as the Red yucca.

PLANTS

A pair of basic gardening terms you'll run across all the time are *Annuals* and *Perennials*. An annual is somewhat like an *ephemera* (**e-fem-ar-ah**), well in a sense it is. An ephemera is an insect, like a May fly, that is born in the morning, breeds in the afternoon and dies at night. Sort of sad when you think about it, isn't it? An annual is the same way only it completes it's life-cycle in a year or less.

You have the seed that germinates, grows, blooms, reseeds itself and dies in but a single growing season. Some examples of annuals are, *Zinnia, African Daisy, Bluebonnet, Marigold, Bachelor's Button, Pansy, Primrose and Phlox.*

A *perennial* is a flowering plant that lives more than two years, most at least three. Some die down in winter but show up again in spring. Perennials usually have fleshy (herbaceous - **herb-bay-shas**) stems and are able to insure a growth the following year through a strong root system that survives most freezes. This herbaceous plant might look dead and done for in winter but it comes back the following year when the summer sun shines new life into it.

Not to confuse you but there is a third one to consider and this is the *biennial* - it lives for two years. Just be certain to ask your friend at your local nursery if the plant is an annual or a perennial then impress them with this biennial term. They'll think you know something even if you don't. Treat gardening like a game and make it fun. It's you against the elements, pests and fungi. Think what a barren world we'd have if it wasn't for grass, plants and trees.

MY TWO FAVORITE LATE-BLOOMING ANNUALS

Larkspur - are mostly background plants that can grow three, maybe four feet high with blue, rose, white or lilac colors. They bloom from May until June. They like sun, rich, loose soil and enjoy being fertilized.

Snapdragon - blooms in red, white, yellow, pink, orange and multi-colors and shows off their stuff from May to June. They like sun but can take a fair amount of shade. They also enjoy water but their leaves do not. They grow to heights from 4 inches to 4 feet. (There is also a Snapdragon *vine* that blooms in blue from May to November.)

THE SUMMER-BLOOMING ANNUALS I LIKE

Dwarf Dahlia (**dale-ya or dal-ya**) - blooms from June to November in a every color imaginable except blue. Likes sun with rich, sandy loam soil, some compost and manure. Grows to about 2 feet high. If seeds are planted in spring you can replant the tubers.

Impatiens (**im-pay-shins**) - Some call them impatients, but you be smart and pronounce them the way they are spelled and if you say it loudly enough you'll have a host of listeners rushing to the dictionary to check you out. These impatiens bloom in red, white, pink and lavender on plants that are as high as two feet and bushy and like sun to light shade.

Marigold flowers look like pom-pons at a football game and grow on stems from a few inches to a few feet tall. These flowers are in yellow and orange and last long when cut, same as the chrysanthemum. Not as impressive to give as roses or lily's but quite lovely for home decorating.

Portulaca (**Poor-choo-lock-ah**) **-** A great plant for your garden to put in front because it grows just to about past your ankle but has flowers in reds, orange, yellow, white and lavender.

Sunflower - You've seen 'em everywhere, I know because they stand out so well. They grow to 9, maybe 10 feet tall and bloom from May to September with big, dinner-plate yellow flowers with a dark center of edible seeds. Parrots as well as kids and most health-food folks love sunflower seeds.

Verbena (**ver-bean-ah**) **-** I know, it's spelled like it's pronounced ver-*ben*-ah but I've also heard it this other way more often. You're in Texas and not a whole lot of things are pronounced like they're written here. There's the Hum-ble building and the city called Um-ble. The street, San Fay-leep-ay is, to Houstonians, San Philip-e. Go with the percentages. You know, like we Texans are always "fixin'" something when it isn't even broke.

Anyway, this plant flowers in violet, red, cream and pastels in clusters on creeping stems. It makes good ground cover or border plant for your garden. You can plant it just about anytime you can buy it and it flowers almost all the time. It's a perennial flower and easy to maintain. Grows maybe a foot high.

Viola, also known as *Johnny jump-up,* blooms from January to May in white, blue, yellow and purple and likes full sun. Excellent bedding plants. Keep faded blossoms picked for new growth. It reaches to maybe 6 inches high.

Zinnia - To sound like you know what you're talking about, you can pronounce it **zin-knee-ah** but if you want to be a "regular" person, most pronounce it **zeen-yah.** You choose. These favorite, easy-to-grow plants come in all sizes and in a truly brilliant array of colors. They like sun, heat and air and deep water at least once a week. You've seen them in most gardens growing on long stalks from one to three feet tall, in full bloom from May to December. Great flowers that make a lively centerpiece.

MY FAVORITE PERENNIALS

Chrysanthemum **(Chris-san-tha-mum) -** Easy to grow and lovely to pick for your dinner table or entryway. The blooms are yellow, orange, purple and white and new varieties are variegated. They like full sun, some water and fertilizer, are hardy and spread easily. They can grow to 3 feet tall with a wing span of as much as 3 feet across.

Coreopsis **(kor-e-opt-sus) -** Also called *Tickseed.* Blooms from May to September showing daisy-like flowers of yellow - orange and grows as high as two feet. Some varieties are smaller and make it to maybe 8 inches high. Some forms are banded. They demand drainage and are tolerant of heat and drought but water them when they look dry.

Daisy - Several varieties but I like the *Bush daisy* best. It blooms year round with the exception of the hot summer months. It likes full sun and demands good drainage. The petals are white, yellow, some salmon and some with violet markings. They bring life to any garden. Also look at the *English daisy* that blooms from January through April and the *Shasta daisy* that blooms from May to November.)

Dianthus - **(Die-an-thuss)** blooms from November to June. A carnation-looking pllant with pink, rose, red, yellow and orange flowers on stems that are maybe 2 feet long. Several varieties such as *Sweet William* (1 to 2 feet high) that bloom for almost 11 months starting in April, the *Wee Willie* (height 4 to 6 inches) bloom from March until June, and the *Magic Charms* that bloom from March to October.

Gerbera - **(jer-bear-ah)** blooms all year long in yellow, orange, coral flame, and red. Likes sun to light shade but protect them from hot sun and cold winters. They are in the daisy family and grow to maybe 18 inches. Likes a 1-2-1 fertilizer and water often but don't make the soil too soggy. (You'll hear me talk about it on my show and I refer it to as the *Gerber* daisy. Maybe I'm thinking about baby food or I just didn't see the "a". Anyway, it's a nice flower.)

Phlox - **(Flocks)** is a large family who mostly like the sun and grow in heights of from 5 inches to 5 feet. The blooms run from white, pink, mauve, salmon and magenta (reddish-purple) to deep red, blue and even a lilac-pink. There are Phlox *(or is in Phloxes, maybe Phloxi)* called *Drummond, Perennial, Prairie, Blue* and *Moss Pink.*

BULBS

Bulbs are plants that store food in swollen underground parts during their dormant season and then when their growing season comes around, they sprout roots, then leaves, and turn into what we call plants. Now, let me impress (maybe boar) you with a few terms many people don't know and fewer care about when planting a garden.

A *true* bulb is like an onion, garlic or lily in that it is made up of fleshy, underground leaves around a short piece of stem. A *corm*, for instance, looks like a bulb but the fleshy part is all stem, like a gladiolus. A *tuber* is also a piece of stem but growth comes from several buds spaced over the surface such as you'll see on some begonias.

A *rhizome* (**rise-ome**) is also a piece of stem that has an elongated shape like an iris root system with new growth coming from the end. Enough of this, you won't remember most of this nohow, right? Let's get on to planting these bulbs and see what wonders they produce.

Most true bulbs bloom in spring, as do tulips, hyacinths and narcissus. Tulips and hyacinths do well in Texas because the weather is not cold for a long period of time to throw them into complete dormancy before the growing season. I suggest you buy these bulbs in early fall and store them in the vegetable bin of your home refrigerator or in that extra refrigerator you have in your garage for a month or so before you plant them.

HERE ARE SOME BULBS THAT I LIKE

Calla Lily - These lovely "old fashioned" flowers grow about 2 to 3 feet tall, depending on the climate and variety. The "cup" of the lily is white with gold, red and pink; a beautiful flower. Plant the bulb in September or October and it will bloom from February to May. Mulch to protect from cold, likes sun or part shade and enjoys taking showers. Fertilize regularly with high phosphate mix.

Crocus - If you plant the bulb in the fall, expect it to bloom from January to March. I'd throw a half-a-handful of bonemeal in a 3 to 4 inch hole and cover it with a few inches of soil. It blooms in white, yellow, orange, lavender and purple and gets about 6 inches high. I'm like the Will Rogers of gardening. I never met a flower I didn't like.

Dahlia - It will bloom from June to November if you plant the bulb in March, April or May. You need to dig a hole about 10 inches deep and fertilize it with that 1-2-1 mixture and don't forget the bonemeal when planting. I talked about it a few pages back in the *Summer-Blooming Annual* category.

Hyacinth - is a hardy bulb that flowers in pink, red, yellow, white, purple and blue. It's best to plant it only 2 to 3 inches deep in the Houston climate in November and December for a spring bloom. I'd space the bulbs 6 to 8 inches apart. They prefer sun.

Another member of the *Hyacinth* family is the **Grape Hyacinth** that you plant in fall to bloom in spring with flowers of both blue and white.

Gladiolus (often called *glad-e-ol-yahs* in the south, not *glad-e-ol-yus,* the correct way) come in every imaginable color. If you plant the bulb from February to September, it blooms from April to June. Plant at about 4 inches deep in rich, sandy garden soil every two weeks and you'll have a bright, pretty, continuous blooming garden.

They like water and sun but many grow under large shade trees that are thinned out to let some sun peek through. The stalks grow from 18 inches to as tall as 5 feet, depending on the species. If you'll notice paintings of Southern Belles standing in their garden with their plantation in the background, you'll notice that they are either holding a bouquet of Gladiolus or you might see these Glad-e-ol-yahs growing in their gardens.

Tulip - A many-colored flower that should be refrigerated 6 to 8 weeks then planted on January first (usually by women since most men are watching the never-ending parade of football games on TV). Enjoys the sun. Bloom in whites, yellows, pinks and reds. Great for the first bloom but in Houston, they just don't make it to bloom number two.

Narcissus - A truly beguiling flower that has quite a story behind it. Do you remember the story of Narcissus from Greek Mythology? He was the guy who was so handsome that he fell in love with his own image. We've all known one Narcissus or other in our lives, haven't we?

Narcissus loved to see his reflection in order to gaze upon his beauty, but in that era, there were no mirrors. So, Narcissus would often go down to a tranquil water hole, crawl out on a limb and look at himself for hours and hours sighing as he looked.

One day, completely self-mesmerized over his good looks, he wanted to get as close to his reflection as possible, maybe to touch it or breathe upon it. He crawled farther out on the limb, causing it to bend more so he could get really close to his flawless face. Crack! The limb broke and dumb Narcissus fell in the water and drowned.

When someone simply adores their own beauty there's a term called **Narcissus Decrepitude**. Loosely interpreted, decrepitude means so "full of yourself" that your thinking is clouded. Narcissus went "overboard" with his self-love, so to speak. Interesting but tragic story, huh? But Greek Mythology seldom has happy endings.

REQUEST: I ask you to indulge me a bit. I've never written a book before and I need some respite to break the arduous task of writing on such a beautiful day when I'd rather be outside playing golf.

Narcissus is the botanical name that means all species and varieties of *daffodils* and *jonquils.* I'll give you a hint on how to have an enviable garden that nobody will be able to figure out. Buy some different bulbs that you like and mix them in a large bucket. Then just toss them into your garden and plant where they fall. Go ahead, take a chance and surprise yourself. It's fun to just take *pot luck* sometimes.

TIP: In planting bulbs that flower, pinch off the dead blooms but never cut the foliage. These bulbs need to make food and the leaves provide it for next years growth.

Houston is truly *Azalea Country* and azaleas don't need as much maintenance as many think. Water them in the summer and when the blooms fall off, fertilize them. Now, where do you plant your azaleas?

Well, you have your trees and shrubs down, your grass is green and healthy and now, where do I plant my azaleas? The answer; just about *anywhere* but on the **west side** of your house where the hot afternoon sun beats against the wall and gives off that reflected heat. It'll burn them down. A good place to plant them is on the *south side* of your house where they will be completely sheltered from that hot afternoon sun. Or the north is okay too - I'm talking about true north and true south.

In caring for azaleas, right after they bloom you fertilize them then wait a month and a half to fertilize again. You don't feed them anymore until after they bloom next year. I know, how much fertilizer, right? The container has excellent instructions and will tell you exactly how much food to put out. They are shallow rooted so you don't want to dig holes in your azalea bed. Just lay the fertilizer on top, take your pruning fork and work it into the soil.

There's liquid and granule azalea food. I like the granules so I can see where I'm putting it and how much. Keep it well watered and prune it right after it blooms. In pruning, just shape it. Sometimes you have something that's called a "sport" that grows wild, it might be 3 feet taller than the rest of the bush. Just clip it back to the bush and shape it to make it pretty. Keep 'em well watered.

If you want a lot of detailed information on azaleas, I'd recommend you go to one of the full-service lawn and garden stores in an around Houston. I like **RCW Nursery**, two miles south of Willowbrook Mall on 249, ask for Tom or Doris, **(713) 440-5161.** These people are professionals.

RCW mixes their own soil and plant food, they have a landscaping department that puts out drawings as well as small booklets and pages of information on azaleas and just about any kind of plant they have in stock. And, if they don't have this information available, they'll find it for you.

ROSE BUSHES

There is *sooo* much to say about roses and azaleas that I yield to the professionals who make their life's work with these two gorgeous plants. So many people love roses and all I can tell you is to - buy the your rose bushes in wintertime. In fact, buy whatever you can in winter because the prices are usually lower and if you can care for them (any and all plants) until spring, you have a deal.

Roses like lots of water and also proper drainage. They don't like wet feet. Prerequisites for producing beautiful roses are raised beds and good sun. Prune your rose bushes in February. You can just water them for a while and about the end of March is when you feed them rose food every month until September, then don't feed them anymore.

Look out for black spot and mildew. Ortho has a good product called *Funginex* that you can use to spray on a weekly basis to keep black spot from coming on your leaf. You have to prevent it from happening. Once you get black spot, you could dip the bush in Funginex and it will only cause the leaves to yellow and fall off. Once they do turn yellow, pull them off the plant or if they fell off, pick them up and throw them away.

Hibiscus come in two basic kind. *Malo* goes down in winter then comes back in spring. *Tropical* are more fragile and if they freeze, they will die. It's best to get these in containers and move them inside during cold spells. Malo produces a huge bloom the size of a saucer or a small dinner plate. The shortcoming of it is that the blooms lasts only one day and fall off, but the blooming *cycle* lasts for several months.

GROUND COVER

People choose ground cover for many reasons; either ordinary grass won't grow because of too much shade, they want to block a short-cut visitors might take, they want to cover protruding tree roots without cutting them, or they just think they look pretty in their garden. I'm going to tell you about only a few of those for the southern climates and you look at the rest on your own.

AJUGA comes in green, bronze or rose-colored leaves with white, blue or cream flowers. It is my favorite ground cover because it vines and spreads, it takes shade well and covers under trees, in gardens and keeps shaded flowerbeds from looking bare and is a hardy plant. Sometimes, you need to thin out this ajuga to get air circulation in and prevent fungal diseases. It likes water and demands good drainage.

MONKEY GRASS is a popular ground cover that seems to be in 1 out of 3 front yards in the south. Just look around and you'll see it somewhere. It's a bulb but I suggest you get it in sprigs and clumps that you can plant maybe 4 to 6 inches apart because it will spread.

Monkey grass takes all sorts of abuse, likes shade better than filtered sun and prefers moist, rich loam. It won't deny water but is *camel-like* in that it can do without it for extended periods. It is a *grass* whose leaves are a dark green and it spreads fast, grows to as high as a foot and is excellent around borders of gardens because it grows thick and keeps the soil from running off flowerbeds.

Direct, hot sun will turn it an unattractive brown. You can buy this grass almost at any nursery but if you look around, your neighbors might be cutting some out or digging it up and they will gladly give it to you. That's the way I've always got mine. I guess it's a perennial too *(or a forever-ennial)* because mine has been in my garden for maybe 8 years and just continues growing and spreading.

CONFEDERATE JASMINE (not to be confused with Carolina JESSamine) is another oft-seen ground cover that can take sun and some shade. It has vine-type runners that spread across the ground and prefers light, sandy acid soil, good drainage and needs to be trimmed and pruned because it will run up drainpipes, brick walls, trees, shrubs, anywhere. It is a dark green with fragrant creamy flowers. I like the Asian Jasmine too. It doesn't grow as tall nor do you need to trim it as much.

IVY - Ahha! This brings back fond memories of my days at Yale - not the university - the Yale *lock repair shop* I worked at in Atlanta that had ivy crawling up, down and sideways over the wet brick fence, up and down the wet brick walls and onto the wet brick patio where we sat on a wet cement bench eating Poor Boy sandwiches for lunch.

There is the *Algerian* and the *English Ivy* that I know of, each with the same characteristics; they both like shade and some sun but some of those rascals grow in full sun. It is another of those plants subject to fungal disease, so don't water them too much.

Their vine-like roots hold to whatever they can feed upon. If they touch the soil, they grab. If they run across a a wet brick wall, they grab on there too. If you can watch it's growth path, you can guide it along the ground and around trees and it is an excellent ground cover. Colors are a green to a dark green with dark red stems.

WANDERING JEW - display small, white flowers on a stem that is dark purple, with leaves of dark green and purple. A hardy plant that spreads quickly in sun or shade, likes water and wants to be fed monthly and grows to maybe 6 inches high. (Many plant them in hanging baskets.)

Wait! Hold your horses! I'm not finished with ground covers just yet. I've only told you about the *living* type. I need to share with you some little secrets on ground cover that won't grow and need little maintenance.

If you already have pines trees let's turn a negative into a positive and put the *pine needles* to work for us. A lot of people who do rake them (folks who don't believe in a bagger) put them around trees to smother any grass or weeds. You can also use chopped up pine needles in your azalea beds or to mulch around other plants you have planted around the house.

Tree bark is another good ground cover around plants. You can buy it in sacks or call a nursery and have it delivered by the truckload, much cheaper that way. Pine bark helps contain the moisture, controls weeds from coming up in your flower beds, and looks pretty good too.

Ground covers are important. First, they are decorative, next they are usually strong enough to eliminate the hint of any weed and third, you don't have to mow in that area.

Again, there's far too many varieties of ground covers to mention any more and the best thing to do is make that trip back to your lawn and garden center and look to see what appeals to you. It's a great way to spend a summer morning and the entire family likes it.

Chapter 6

LAWN AND GARDEN MAINTENANCE

COMMON LAWN DISEASES

Black Sooty Mold usually comes on the tips of St. Augustine grass. It's got that salt and pepper look, that's the *precursor,* the fore mass for that slime mold that will eventually form. The best thing to do is to take a garden hose and wash it off then mow your lawn. When the temperature and the conditions get wrong, that's when fungal diseases show their faces.

When you see a *Fairy Ring* of mushrooms pop up in your yard in a circle, this means the spore was there but the temperature and conditions and humidity got just right and the spores grew into mushrooms. Don't worry about trying to kill mushrooms. If you play golf, I recommend a 7-Iron. Just get out there and swing away with that golf club and knock 'em down or take your rake and rake them down. Some mushrooms are poisonous and small kids will eat almost anything. Just knock them down or rake them and they'll go away until the next time these conditions are just right to knock 'em down again. They're easy to detect.

I guess everyone who ever had a lawn is familiar with the words *Brown Patch*. It can be prevented by putting out a *systemic fungicide* with *Baleyton* before it shows itself. You can do this only by experience. If Brown Patch occurred in October of last year, treat your yard in September of this year. Use *Daconil, Consan or Terrichlor* to stop the spread of brown patch. Terrichlor seems to last the longest, maybe 3 months, all through the winter. Don't panic! There's a difference between *dead* and *ugly*. Your grass is only ugly, not dead, and will grow back in the springtime.

Yellow Patch is about the same, just Brown Patch with a yellow tinge. Don't fertilize and use these same fungicides to treat it. There are some fungi that are everywhere. One is called the *Devil's Snuff Box* and another was called the *Postman's Disease*. A mail carrier would pick up a fungus on his shoes in one yard then spread it through yard after yard over his entire postal route. Soon the entire city would have the same fungus on their lawns.

I think the smart thing to do if you see a fungus growth and you aren't certain what it is, get a ziploc bag and clip off a few leaves and get them to your nurseryman. He can tell much better with a sample than if you try to describe it to him in words like "kind of dark and dusty" of "slimy and greenish" or "fuzzy and it doesn't smell too good."

SAD (**St. Augustine Decline**) is a viral disease that shows up as a mottling on the blades of your St. Augustine in a grayish or yellowish color. There is no known cure. I suggest you cut around the area and dig it up and plug in new St. Augustine grass.

You would fall off your milk bucket with laughter if you heard some of the descriptions we get. In fact, if you listen to our program you'll know what I mean. Some people have called in the show and actually held up a leaf or a bug in front of their telephone and say, "It looks like this."

MOWING

I say cut your lawn the way you like. If you want your grass to be 2 inches high and you cut it every Saturday, if it's 3 inches tall by Friday, guess you'll have to cut it more often, won't you?

To prevent your grass from getting all chewed up, always keep your mower blades sharpened and cut the grass higher in summer than in winter. I know this isn't any fun because this means you will have to cut it more often. (I beg your pardon. I never promised you a rose garden. Now why did I say that? That's the second reference I've made to a song and I am not musically inclined).

There are differing opinions as to whether to leave the grass clippings on your lawn to add organic matter. Well, the mulching mower cuts the grass up so fine that it probably does add to the overall plant health and growth, but I've seen people who hadn't cut their grass in a few weeks leave the grass on their lawn and it turned it brown and killed the live grass it was resting on. Some say if you cut your grass once a week, rake it every *second* week and that makes sense except I hate to rake. I think the mulching mower is the answer. I like 'em!

WATERING YOUR LAWN

Plants as well as people can live without food but we all need water. I'll explain when and how much to water but I need to also tell you about some methods you might choose other than my way; standing out in the yard with a hose.

Sprinkler Systems: All sprinkler systems need underground pipes which means digging with a shovel or using a long blade on your edger and then digging a bit deeper with your shovel. It isn't that difficult to do yourself because the PVC pipe is easy to work with.

Go to a store that has a Sprinkler System display and ask questions from someone there who knows. It will help estimate the cost if you bring a diagram (and measurements) of your yard, same as you do with your nursery drawing.

There are several types of sprinkler heads and most of them pop up when the system is turned on. Some people prefer the older type that are level with the ground and there are the sprinkler tubes that stick above the ground used to water plants and/or shrubs in a flowerbed or where you won't be using your lawn mower. The displays will be there for you to see and there are always brochures for you to read before you decide.

There are a number of *stationary sprinklers* you'll see everywhere. The simplest type is the one that can water in square or rectangular patterns on your lawn that is shown to the right.

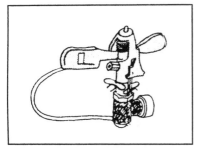

Here's a picture of an *Impulse sprinkler* that actually shoots out water through a small nozzle that is then deflected by a spring-loaded arm.

Then, there's this *Oscillating sprinkler* that uses a perforated spray head tube which causes the sprinkler to oscillate slowly from side to side. The distance it reaches depends upon the individual sprinkler.

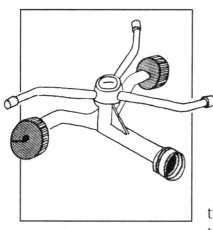

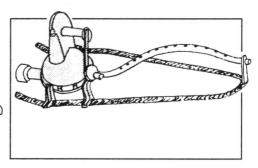

Here's a *Revolving sprinkler* that shows two "arms" parallel to the ground that rotate and disperse water through nozzles at the ends of each arm.

Many people are going to the *Soaker hose* that allows water to seep out all along the length of the hose that will deep-water right to the roots. It is made of a porus rubber and the degree it leaks is controlled by the density of the rubber. You've seen them and know what they are.

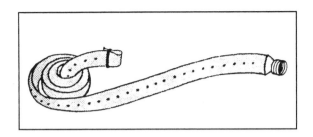

Another method is with the *Drip hose* that has tiny holes throughout the entire length. This hose is plastic and flat where you can roll it up like a small version of a fire hose and then spread it out on your lawn. Little sprinkles of water shoot up and out in all directions so hook one on to a length of solid garden hose and drag it around to where you need it. Or, let it soak and move it when the area is wet to your satisfaction.

Most folks who can afford it are going for an automatic watering system. There are types on the market that will do exactly what you want them to do. Thing is, this Texas weather is sri totally unpredictable that it might be dry for weeks or even months then rain like the dickens for a few days or weeks without letup. I've seen it (and so have you) when an automatic watering system is up and pouring during a heavy rain. There are, however, the more sophisticated systems that shut off when the ground is wet.

I don't know whether it's being old, old-fashioned or cheap, but I use a regular garden hose with a few different nozzles and sprinkler heads, one type for my front yard, one for the side of my house and an oscillating sprinkler for my back yard.

I water from the top, water when I need to water and I drag the hose. I know the books say to water in the morning only to discourage diseases, but I don't like getting *up* in the morning and usually, the water pressure is low because everybody reads the same book. If I gettup early and it's a good day for watering, I go to the nearest golf course.

I say water morning *or* evening. I usually water my front yard in the evening simply because that's when it's convenient for me to do it. Many will argue the point that it's not good to water your St. Augustine late a night or in the late afternoon because the water sits on the roots overnight and it causes fungal diseases. If that is true, *Mother Nature* must be in the *fungicide* business on the side and has operated all wrong because every morning when I get up to get the paper and walk through the grass, I swear but it's always wet.

I think a person needs to water their grass when it's convenient to them. Sun is not going to hurt your grass with water on it, you'll just have more evaporation. I wouldn't advise, however, that you water in late morning or early afternoon or when the sun is high above because it will burn your grass. But morning or evening, I can't see a major difference. It's worked okay for me for...well, over several decades.

Many people time their sprinkler systems set to go on early in the morning before they get up and it's done for them. Some water in the middle of the day. Golf courses, for instance, water almost *all* the time and surely they must know what is right or wrong with their grass and how to care for it.

Too, you need a certain amount of pressure for that sprinkler system to work properly and if everybody waters in the morning, where is the pressure? People are getting up bathing, boiling water and some water their lawns and you might have a drip coming out of your sprinkler.

These automatic sprinkler systems might impress your visiting relatives but they are often timed to go on regardless of the weather and if there's a flood outside, there's no need to water so you have to go out and shut it off and then put it back on manually. I like 'em but they aren't foolproof.

If I was going to water my grass with a sprinkler system I'd have it set to come on for say 30 minutes and then I'd check it. If I have run off, I'd set it back and if I didn't, I'd set it for maybe 10 minutes longer. You don't want water to run down to the curb (but just about to that point) and then have that timed sprinkler shut itself off.

If you water thoroughly and deeply, there's no need to water more than once a week. The whole basis of this watering stuff is to make the root system support and produce a healthy plant. You want the roots to grow deep. If you water lightly, the roots will try to reach up for this moisture and become subject to all sorts of problems with insects and diseases. The deeper the root, the more hardy the plant.

Thorough and infrequent watering is best, say watering every 4 or 5 days. How often and how much you water depends on your soil, the annual rainfall, the humidity, and the condition of your grass. It will tell you when it needs water or if you've watered too much.

Chapter 7

WEEDS AND CHINCH BUGS

The true definition of a weed is "anything you don't want growing in your garden." In general, there are 2 kinds of weeds, *broad leaf* and *narrow leaf* weeds. There's broadleafweed killer that will eliminate the weeds. The narrow leaf weeds have the same genetic makeup as our grass so if you try to *kill* this narrow leaf weed, like Nut grass, with a weed killer, you would kill all grasses in that area.

There is a product on the market called *Weed Block* that looks like black plastic but it is porus and allows water and nutrients to bleed through yet it stops the weeds. You can put this near the top of your garden, maybe a half inch or inch of soil over it to hide the material and it will stop the weed seeds from pushing up. Cut holes in it to plant trees or shrubs or tomato plants. It's about 3 feet wide and comes in 50 foot rolls and you can get it at almost any garden center and it lasts more than one season.

A cheap remedy for weeds is by taking the *Chronicle* or the *Post* and spreading the newspaper out over the area. When this paper decomposes it forms a mulch. The scientific approach of ridding a garden or lawn of weeds is with weed killers. They are two main categories; the *pre-emergents prevent* the weeds from coming in and the *post-emergents* kill existing weeds.

Grass family weeds are like *Johnson grass, Crab grass and Goose grass.* When trying to get rid of a weed, do not cut the grass for a few days before or after applying a weed killer. Broadleaf weeds are killed quicker in temperatures of from 60-70 degrees and for grass weeds, 70-75 degrees. Post emergents work best on sunny days.

A general rule for pre-emergent weed killers is to make one application in early spring and another in late summer. Remember to water these pre-emergent weed killers just after putting them on your lawn. Do not use weed killers on a new lawn, wait at least for the second growing season.

Ferti-lome, a co-op gardening group, has a Lawn and Garden Guide you can pick up free at your nursery. In it is a complete description of their products, prices, amounts and applications for caring for your lawn and garden.

I also recommend all the *Ortho* and *Green Light* products. As time and scientific knowledge gathers, we are getting better and better at being able to solve lawn and garden problems. Just read the labels, talk to your nurseryman or to a knowledgeable person at your lawn and garden center and they will direct you.

Knowing what to look for and being aware of the problems *before* they occur is the answer. "One bag (or bottle) of prevention is worth a dead lawn of cure." Now that doesn't make a whole lot of sense, does it? See what happens when I try to get cute and bend popular quotations but you get the idea, don't you?

Become a student at this, because knowledge in everything is the answer. I'm hoping to put you in the *get-up-and-do-it* mode and offer these guidelines. If you have a specific problem, gather a sample of whatever it is that bothers you about your growing greenery and put it in that little baggie I talked about and take it along with you to your nursery. If they don't know the answer, take it to a nurseryman (woman) who does.

Crab grass is a narrow leaf weed and there are herbicides on the market that will keep crab grass from coming out. When it gets in your St. Augustine grass, you can't put grass killer on it because it'll kill the good grass and you can't paint each narrow leaf with this stuff. When these unwanted grasses first begin to peek out, the only way I found is to dig them out with a spade.

Stickers? A weed we find in unfertile soil, much on the Gulf Coast area and the closer you get to Galveston, you'll find them growing in the St Augustine. If you want to get rid of these stickers, fertilize and get the grass to become stronger than these weeds. The **19-5-9** *Easy Gro Premium* will provide enough strength for your St. Augustine that it will choke out many of these problems.

There are different formulations for different plants. Roses, for instance, need different fertilizer than St. Augustine grass. I hate to keep saying "go to your local lawn and garden store" or "talk to your nurseryman about it" but that is truly the best way. These stores and these people are in an area they are familiar with and can advise you accordingly. They also have the up-to-date treatment for everything.

These are some rules to follow to keep weeds from invading your lawn or garden:

1. **They both need adequate water.**
2. **Your lawn needs regular mowing.**
3. **The must both be fertilized.**
4. **Mulch your garden.**
5. **Rake or mulch-cut your lawn.**
6. **They both need sunshine.**
7. **Aerate your lawn if necessary.**

And # 8, not trying to be corny or repeat myself but, "The best thing to put over your lawn and garden is your shadow!" If you watch over what is going on you'll have most of the problems solved before they occur.

Weeds on a lawn are no big problem because with proper care (watering, fertilizing and cutting) the grass will take over and the weeds will be snuffed out. I hate weeds that invade my *flower* or *vegetable* garden because weeds steal the nutrients, take up moisture and serve as a haven for pests and diseases. Too, they multiply and starve the plants even more.

Remember what I said was the description of a weed? My St. Augustine grass, for instance is not a weed is it? You say *no* and I say *yes*. We're both right! It isn't a weed in your lawn but it certainly is a weed in my garden! Why? Because I don't want it there!

CHINCH BUGS

When it gets hot and dry in the summertime, these marauders will kill your lawn faster than anything else. These darn bugs will attack the stems of your St. Augustine grass and suck it dead. The best way to guard against them is to have a healthy lawn that is well-watered and with soil that is not nitrogen deficient. Also, to treat your lawn with Dursban or Diazinon, either in liquid or granule form.

Chinch bugs are especially lethal during hot summers. They like dry, unfertilized grass. When you identify the chinch bug, the best thing to do right then is to spray them with *Dursban* and send them to chinch bug heaven.

For instance, if you're driving home and notice a neighbor's yard that is turning brown, this is a signal to look for chinch bugs in your own yard. Go to the *Dursban*. In this instance I like the liquid because I like to see the stuff get on the bugs and the instant the liquid touches him, bye-bye. With the granules, it oftentimes has to be activated with water. I like the fast stuff for these nuisances or mankind.

Get a sprayer, mix the Dursban with water, and spray. Now, don't spray the area where they've been! That's dead and if it's dead there is no amount of fertilizer, insecticide or prayer to bring it back to life. Spray the areas around the dead areas. The green stuff is where they're at so, cut 'em off at the pass! The best way to repair this is to dig under the spot and clear it then sprig it with St. Augustine.

I advise again, for you to go to your area lawn and garden store and look at the various chemicals that are manufactured *especially for you* and for *your problems.* Go to your nursery and look up these products also or talk with your nurseryman about what it is you need to know.

I know it sounds like a cop out when I say to visit a nursery or a lawn and garden store but in reality, it's the blamed truth. My hope for this book is to enlighten you on many of the things you need to ask so you won't be completely naive when talking to your nurseryman. They will be able to serve you faster and better once you have read this book. They might even enjoy talking with you because you'll know some of what you need to ask and, hopefully, know how to ask it.

Too, this is your handy reference guide to tell you *what, when, where*, and *how.* The rest you have to search out the way I'm telling you. I get calls again and again, many of the time the same calls, and the same caller who forgot what I said, or didn't write the entire information down, or didn't know how to spell whatever products I advised.

Others say they understand the advice but in reality, they don't. So, they call back again and again. I'm hoping if they buy this book, that it answers their question(s) then I can get on to other callers with new problems and also have time to I can get on with my second book.

I really do enjoy answering your questions. Whatever the answer is you need, I don't mind you calling. It's because of your calls that I have a job.

Chapter 8

"CIDES"

Let's get rid of the ants, fleas, poison ivy, poison oak, fungal diseases and all the other little bugs and flies and mites that suck and eat our grass, kill our plants and make our lives miserable. Let's find out how to keep our lawns and plants and trees healthy and be able to enjoy our yards and gardens.

If that's all you want to do and that will make you happy, you're turned to the right chapter. I call it "Cides" because they are all in a general group called Pesticides that we break down to *Herbicides, Fungicides* and *Insecticides.*

1. **Herbicides kill vegetation.**
2. **Fungicides kill fungus.**
3. **Insecticides kill insects.**

To make certain there are no mistakes when dealing with pesticides, be sure to read the label on whatever pesticide you buy. Manufacturers spend millions of dollars on research to get the information they condense for you and print on their label. Spend a few minutes and read before you put anything on your grass or flowers.

HERBICIDES

We "touched on" herbicides the chapter before when dealing with chinch bugs, but there's more to say. What about herbicides for unwanted grass and weeds? Our big answer is *Roundup Grass & Weed Killer.* It seems to be a name almost everybody knows.

It will kill all things; St. Augustine grass, vegetable plants, weeds, small trees, vines bushes, poison ivy, everything that grows! It is a *Systemic Herbicide.* When it gets on the green leaf surface and then moves down the stem to the root system it stops the formation of certain amino acids found only in plants.

People use it for grass that grows between cracks in their sidewalk, driveway, patio, around building foundations, in rock flower beds where the grass often peeks through or to completely kill out a diseased lawn and ready it for replanting. Farmers spray around their fencelines to kill vines, poison ivy and poison oak, sticker bushes and other unwanted weeds. It is a powerful weed and grass killer.

Roundup is best to spray on during the warmest part of the day, preferably when the temperature is between 65 and 85 and when it doesn't look like it will rain for 7 or 8 hours.

It is excellent for preparing new vegetable gardens in that you can spray it on, wait until the grass dies, then till it. It is not harmful to any plant after it has been down 7 days and the grass and weeds it kills begins to yellow after 3 days. It isn't necessary to drench the plant and when the spray dries, it is not harmful to pets or pests. For the few weeds that might reappear, hit them with another shot of spray.

For small patios and gardens you can purchase the ready-mixed spray. It is for the person who has but a few worrisome weeds popping up here and there and doesn't want to fool around with mixing. For larger areas, you'll need the *concentrate* or *super concentrate* and the label will tell you how much to mix and how much area it will cover.

A product I like for selective weeding is *Weed-B-Gon.* You simply spray it on your St. Augustine and kill the lawn-invading broad leaf weeds. For Nutgrass and Crabrass, I like *Kleenup,* systemic grass and weed killer. If you don't keep your lawn healthy, these are products that forgive you.

Green Light has a product called *Wipe Out,* an excellent, systemic broad leaf weed killer. None of these is harmful to humans or pets but while spraying, wear goggles, gloves, long sleeve shirts and pants and if you get any of this spray on you, just to be safe, wash it off with water.

It is especially important to wear this protective gear when walking through weeds and brush to ward off poison ivy, poison oak or poison sumac. Helps with keeping stickers off and blackberry bush "arms" from reaching you too. If a thorny arm from one of these sticker bushes gets around your ankle, your body will come to an abrupt halt.

When mixing *any* herbicide, read those directions on the label. You can mix a stronger solution for these hard-to-kill areas or to speed up the pace of the devastation they'll cause. This concentrate *can* irritate your skin so wear that protective covering.

Also, never apply any herbicide when it's windy. You don't want this stuff to blow from a weed you're trying to kill to your rose bushes or to blow over to a neighbors lawn and do irreparable damage.

FUNGICIDES

A Fungicide is for things like *Powdery mildew, Brown patch, Gray leaf spot, Dollar spot* and *Grease spot*, among others. Sometimes on roses or Crape Myrtles especially, you'll get something that looks like a little white powder on the leaves. To get it off, I use *Consan Triple Action 20.* Mix it up, spray it on and it will wash right off. It's the fungicide I would use. The white powder comes off immediately. Some people wash it off with a garden hose and water, and if that works for you, do it. I just happen to like a chemical agent to help that water along.

Daconil is a multi-purpose fungicide for everything from Brown Patch in your front yard to fungal problems in your flower or vegetable garden. Fungal problems can be prevented by spraying a fungicide as a precautionary measure before evidence of a problem arises.

This is the plan. Find out what you have that is hurting your lawn. Get down on your hands and knees and pluck a sample or two of the grass that is affected by a mold or mildew and put it in a little baggie to bring to your nursery. Or look for these bugs, and if possible, do the same thing. Then, you'll know what product to buy and in what strength. The Dursban granules, for instance, come in a variety of strengths, all marked clearly on the package.

INSECTICIDES

This term is self-explanatory - it is the "cide" that kills insects. Let's begin with the biggest problem found on most lawns that is not only a bother but is also painful when they bite - **FIRE ANTS!** Over a period of years, I have tried everything and I have friends who have tried everything.

I've known people who used gasoline on ants because it seems to do the trick whereas all it will do is kill the ants on top, kill your grass at the same time, and make a toxic waste dump in your yard. Men like doing this, gives them that *Rambo* feeling. Yeah, they put on an old torn shirt and wrap a bandanna around their head, rub a little grease paint on their cheeks and are ready for war.

In ridding your lawn of ants, the *queen* is the key; get her and you get the mound. But she is hiding way below in safety and the only way to get her other than a bulldozer or back hoe, is to fool these worker ants into not brushing their feet on a welcome mat and tracking the poisoned powder to the queen and the rest of the mound.

Books and ant pamphlets say, *"When she dies, the mound dies."* I can't imagine that. Do they all come into contact with the powder? Do the ones that don't, die of a lonely heart because their queen died? Do they have a mass suicide pact? I think the survivors probably go to your neighbor's yard or to another section of your own yard and rebuild.

I'll share some of my ant knowledge with you at this point. First, the queen ant is the only one who lays eggs. There might be two or more queens in one mound and you have to get them all. She can lay as many as 600 eggs a day. When she dies, there are no more eggs thus, in a period of several days, she and any other ants who tramped though this poison succumb.

One of the best products for eliminating fire ants quickly is *Orthene.* I put a little on a teaspoon and sprinkle Orthene on the mound in the early morning or late afternoon when the ants are active and let the dumb ants bring it to their queen. In a single day, the ants are gone! You don't need to circle the mound or spray it with water.

There are "deal" packages of fire ant treatment that really look good. *"Why spend 5 or 6 dollars for such a small can or this when I can get this **big** package for the same price?"* Well friends and neighbors, it isn't the same! Read the label. I've seen folks use a hundred pounds of those large packs of this so-called fire ant killer and all it does is run them into other areas of your yard. No sir, get the queen and *Orthene* does it best. *Amdro* also has a bait that kills them. I've had excellent results with both.

Another fire ant killer used with good results by many of my callers is *Organic Plus.* It has a pyrethrum in it, a quick, non-residual killer of ants that will get rid of a fire ant mound quickly. Also, a lot of people are having good luck with *Dursban granules* that they put on their lawns to discourage these ants from ever choosing their front yard as a building site. Yes, prevention is the smart way to go.

Dursban works as a control treatment for all sorts of insects that could invade your garden. Look at the label on the *Dursban Lawn & Garden Insect Control* packet and be impressed. It impressed me!

It takes care of surface feeding pests such as *Sod Webworms, Armyworms, Crickets, Grasshoppers, Fleas* and *Ticks*, as well as soil insects like *Grubworms* and *Soil Crickets.* If you have and vegetable plants in your front yard, it will prevent an invasion of *Wireworms, Cutworms, Root Maggots* and *Billbugs.*

This amazing formula also kills home-invading pests such as *Ants, Cockroaches, Earwigs, Sowbugs, Silverfish and Spiders.* I used the insect spray for my storage shed and corners in my garage that seem to lure spiders and webs. It's just an eerie feeling, isn't it, to walk into a web and have it clutch to your hair and around your face? Squirt 'em!

The Dursban spray on plants controls the sucking insect pests such as aphids as well as ants. Again, read that label and see if that particular spray or dust or granule is what you need to get rid of what you don't want.

The *Carpenter Ant* is black or reddish-black, some have wings and some just crawl. They're a bit faster than other ants maybe because they're bigger and have longer legs. They can do damage to the wood around the foundation of your home, garage or workshop. To stop this, spray with *Ortho-Klor*, a potent soil insect and termite killer.

I'm not getting paid or bought a free lunch from the people at Ortho, it's just that they are resolute in their pursuit of just about everything that needs to be tended to with your lawn, home, or garden. Their displays and products are in the lawn and garden section in most stores. They also have a complete set of brochures and books available.

If you need further explanation on Ortho products, they have a staff of friendly and courteous experts who seem happy to help. Call their toll-free number any weekday from 8:30 AM until 5 PM. **1-800-225-2883.**

Another ant that seems to always be around is the little *Pharaoh ant.* They might start outside but they come inside quickly enough. Some people call them "Sugar ants" and some call them" "Piss ants." Whatever name they go by doesn't matter, they are pests that are not easy to control.

They form colonies near, at and under your house and get inside your wall via the electric wiring that they use as highways. They'll walk along inside the walls and baseboards then show up in the kitchen, bathroom, anywhere. They like sugars, carbohydrates and chicken fat and seem to walk along in a never-ending line. Push them with your thumb and more follow. Push again, and still more follow.

The *only* way Pharaoh ants can be controlled (a nice word for kill) is with bait. If they take this poison bait back to the colony, it does the job. All the mashing or swatting is to no avail, they just keep coming and coming in that long, never-ending line. Topical insecticides will cause a break in this long line but it will not, in the words of Arnold Schwartzenegger, "Terminate them!"

Pharaoh ants are the biggest headache for a pest control man because it takes almost a full month after the ants get the poison bait before they all die. The technician will tell the homeowner that it will take time but they know the homeowner will call back a time or two because one month seems like a long time. They just grin and bear it.

I like *Big State Pest Control* company best. They advertise on my show, they answer all my questions, they help the people I ask to call them, I use them, and I recommend them highly. If you have that problem now, call Big State at **(713) 667-3787** or dial **NO PESTS.** No need to write down or remember this number now. I have them all listed for your convenience in the back of this book.

If Big State is not in your area, just about any pest control company is okay as long as they are reputable and stand behind their work. The prices vary only slightly depending on the location and how nice their building is.

Being conservative, I'd try the inexpensive method first, by using some of what I recommend that you can buy at the store and see what it does. Sometimes the problem is so severe that you'll need a professional. Call them!

FLEAS AND OTHER CRITTERS

For those of you who would like to rise a degree or two above the majority of the population and who would like to learn more about fleas, let me tell you some things most people don't know (or care about). It could make a fun topic of discussion with your neighbor when you're leaning against the back fence in idle conversation. I don't suggest this at a cocktail or dinner party but if you happen to be in a back yard barbecue and the subject comes up, overwhelm those in hearing distance with this newly-found knowledge.

Fleas work in a 4-cycle stage that start with the *egg;* they hatch in 1 or 2 days. Then, there's the flea *larva* that feeds from 4 to 8 days, followed by the *pupa* that the larva spins into a cocoon and in 5 days, the *adult* flea emerges. An adult flea can live 2 years without feeding.

This bit of news won't help you much other than if you can "get" this booger in the first three stages, you've saved some bites as well as a population increase. You see, fleas lay from as many as 6000 eggs at a single time.

Dr. Bart Drees, head of the Texas A&M Department of Entomology, is the area expert on ants and fleas, but I can't reach him until tomorrow and I need to get this book out tonight. I will however, in my next book, find out more about fleas and share that information with you. Until then, in the words of Paul Harvey, "Then you'll know, the rest of the story."

Fleas are a major problem especially during the summer because fleas and ticks get on your animals and if the animals are in the house, the fleas could very well take over. To prevent this, treat your yard, your animals and your house, preferably all at the same time, but in that order.

A few weeks before the weather gets warm in your area, get *Dursban* granules, scatter them with your Broadcast spreader to *prevent* and *discourage* fleas and other insects from coming into your yard.

Fleas like moist areas that are protected from direct sun and sunlight. If your dog or cat doesn't sun bathe all the time, they probably have a favorite area under a tree, alongside the house or in the garage where they sleep. In those areas, *spray* Dursban *liquid* liberally.

Hoping you can put your pets in the garage while you're treating your yard, treat them next, same day if you can. There are a number of flea and tick-control products for animals, but before using any of the strong type, I say take your pet(s) to the vet. Some breed of dogs and cats are sensitive to these insecticides and, I know you love these animals and want to be sure. If your pet has a favorite resting spot inside your home or a bed of their very own, be certain to spray that area also - after you wash the bedding.

This is a difficult problem to solve. If your pets just wander outside your home, they'll pick fleas up from other lawns or other animals and bring them home - outside on your lawn and inside your house. You almost *do* have to go to war against these bothersome pests.

For inside your home, vacuum your carpets, rugs and furniture and wash your bedding and sheets. There are various foggers on the market that might work well in small areas. If you haven't any time to clean and spray as I advised and need a quick-fix, the spray might suffice but I'd go after them with the big guns.

I've heard excellent reports on a product called *Dursban LO,* put down in spray form. Spray it on your carpet, furniture and drapes. Now, the Dursban LO kills the adult fleas but you'll also need *Precor* mixed with your Dursban LO to get to the small fleas and the eggs. This will work for up to three months.

Ortho's *Total* has Precor and they say one treatment will last for 210 days. If your cat or dog doesn't relish being sprayed, try *Sevin Garden Dust* on them. Remember to cover your pets eyes while spraying or dusting the little loves.

I didn't mean to neglect the *tick,* but ticks are controlled in the same manner as fleas, what works on one usually works on the other. If you have a tick problem and the Dursban doesn't work, call that Ortho hotline and find out what they say about it. They're the experts.

Yet another bothersome pest is the *cockroach,* especially when they come uninvited into your home. Come to think of it, I can't recall one person who ever actually *invited* them in so I guess we need to get rid of them outside before they come in. Yeah, *La Cucaracha* is a lively song but a big, dark roach is not pleasant to see crawling up a wall, across your floor or sounding like an army inside your pantry.

The *mucho grande* ones are the tree roach - the *American Cockroach*. They (usually) stay outside but when it gets cold and wet, like anything else, it will seek warmth and come inside the house. They try to squeeze under the front door, get in through your shingles or come down the chimney; they're innovative intruders.

One of my favorite things to use to spray for cockroach elimination is *Red Circle's* **Powerhouse!** It's safe to spray anywhere, and is safe to use around kids and pets. It is *sooo* powerful that you take this aerosol can and squirt it in your pantry or around the baseboards in your home and if a roach should stumble on to this stuff by accident, *c'est la vie!*

If you see a cockroach walking through while you're reading this book, you can either step on them or hit them with the book. But these giant cockroaches will only walk away with the book on their back. Maybe a Yellow Pages will do it. I'd use the Powerhouse and just sweep them up in the morning with a dustpan.

With Aphids and White flies...It's easiest to get these critters when they're small. When you see the first insects on a leaf, usually on the tender growth parts, spray. Sprays to chose from are Orthene, Dursban, Diazanon and Malethion.

Chapter 9

PRUNING AND TRANSPLANTING

TREES

Many yards would be greatly "dressed up" simply by cutting a few tree branches and pruning some hedges and maybe shaping some of the plants. It's easy to do and truly will make a difference in how well your garden looks (or doesn't look). To me, a yard that is not pruned looks about as good as a guy who never gets a haircut.

The key to pruning is to make the tree or bush look natural. The reasons for pruning are many. For instance, most people prune to cut off dead limbs or branches to shape their tree or bush. You can also either restrain or promote growth of a plant by pruning. If you cut it, it stands to reason that it won't grow taller and if cut correctly, it could grow taller.

By trimming branches from a tree, it allows the sun to come through thereby adding more life and color to your grass or plants. And by pruning some vegetable plants and fruit trees, you get larger and healthier fruit.

There are certain times to prune various trees and shrubs and you need to learn when. Deciduous plants, for example, are best pruned in spring before they begin to flower. Evergreen should be pruned and shaped when they are small to prevent any drastic cutting later on. The narrow-leaf evergreens are best if pruned in April.

A simple rule is if the branch is dead, cut it off. If you are pruning because a certain branch is diseased, be certain to wash those shears in a water/clorox mixture before pruning (and infecting) healthy branches.

In cutting tree limbs that are high up or if you have a lot of them, it's far better to call a professional. If it's limbs that you can easily reach, be sure to position that ladder *behind* the large tree. I've seen many a do-it-yourselfer knocked down from a tree or have the limb fall on something else causing much more damage than the price they'd have paid to a tree company.

For smaller limbs, you can clip most of those with the lopping shears or a small tree saw and then paint the open wound with a regular tree paint. Cut as close to the trunk or main branch as you can.

If you're using a chain saw or regular saw, make the first cut on the *underside* of the limb and not too close to the trunk. It will prevent the limb from falling down and tearing bark from the main tree.

Make the second cut on the top of the limb and a little bit in front of the under cut so the limb will break without damage of stripping. On your final cut, make it close to the trunk and afterwards, coat it down or spray it with the tree paint you can get at most stores. This makes the job look professional and prevents any diseases.

For cutting tree roots, such as girdling roots, you've seen 'em, the ones that wrap around every which way at the base of a tree, use a saw or sharpshooter and just cut 'em as close to the trunk as you can and coat it with the preservative tree paint.

For roots that are under your walkway or driveway, I'd get a shovel and get down to the root and cut it off too. Remember, if you use a chain saw, have an extra blade or two handy. The second that chain, moving at that high rate of speed touches dirt, it will dull it almost instantly. I'd use whatever I could; ax, sharpshooter, hand saw and chain saw. If you cut off too many of these large roots, you might endanger the life of the tree.

This is when you choose between having *speed bumps* running across your drive breaking cement, or a tree that shouldn't have been planted there in the first place? I say cut away and get a new, more sensible tree for that spot.

If you have a pecan tree in your front yard, don't prune it, just cut the lower limbs so you can mow under it. With pecan trees, if you cut it you only stunt the growth and halt the nut production. You can prune oak or ash trees which is referred to as grooming or shaping. Cut off competitive branches that cross over each other or that grow wild. Cut the top branch or any wayward branch.

HEDGES AND SHRUBS

In pruning or trimming hedges or shrubs, just make certain you cut the limb that is broken, dead or that you want removed, as close to the main limb as possible. In pruning, you are sending a signal to the main plant that you want new growth and that you are helping to keep it healthy.

Always cut just above the bud or a healthy side branch. Prune close to the main branch and never leave any long stubs. Cut off long shoots to shape your tree and know that new growth will grow below that cut. Trim (or prune) branches that grow over and rub against the other.

An *espalier* (I don't know how to pronounce that, I've heard it pronounced by different professionals as *s-pal-ear, s-pal-yay* and *s-pal-yar*) is a trellis or frame used to train small trees to grow a certain way. *Espaliering* is training a plant to grow in the shape or direction you choose.

People do it with tomato plants by putting up wiring, encircling them in a wire cage and/or by putting in stakes next to them and tieing small insulated wire to the plant. Fruit trees are done in a similar fashion. This diagram shows how.

Another form of pruning is by *pinching* a plant. If you want a plant to grow tall, pinch off growth tips on all side branches. To cause it to grow wider and bushier, pinch off the tips of the plant so it will spread.

Plants have little growths that spring up between the main stalk and a side limb called *suckers*. Perhaps the slang phrase, "Get out of here you little sucker", was formulated by a gardener who was pinching of these little offshoots from his tomato plants. Regardless, when these suckers are removed from tomato plants, the plants grow better fruit.

These little suckers also show up at the *base* of trees. If so, pruning will only encourage more growth so it's necessary to dig down and cut them off *right at the trunk* and coat them with tree paint. Don't worry about damaging the tree itself, it will survive and grow healthier without these little offshoots that are bothersome.

Pruning shears and lopping shears both do the same thing but the long handles give you better reach. There is also a long-handled device called a *pole pruner* for cutting high limbs in trees.

If a plant or shrub seems dead, it just might be. To be sure, wait until spring. If it's dead now it'll still be dead in spring. To make certain, make a thin cut with a pocket knife and if the bark still shows white, it is alive. Try to water and fertilize it back to health. If it's all brown, it's dead.

TRANSPLANTING TREES

The easiest way of transplanting a tree is the telephone. Just call **Foster Tree Service** at **(713) 458-5992.** A tree, per se, is a large item and it needs professional handling. I'm referring to, of course, a tree that is maybe 15 or more feet tall with a trunk that is 5 to 6 inches in diameter. That's just too darn big for a person or two (or three) to handle.

If you have a smaller tree, say one you plan to dig up from somewhere to plant in your yard, one that is say 10 or so feet tall with a trunk of maybe 2 or 3 inches in diameter, you can do this with help. Or if you have a similar sized tree you want to *move* from one spot in your yard to another, that's possible without calling any nursery or tree service.

It's sort of a Catch 22, in that I recommend you don't dig up a tree on your own that is smaller than say 6 or so feet but then if it's too big, it is truly difficult. But if you have a tree that is a few years old, not too tall or with too thick a trunk, here's what you do.

Call any reputable tree service company and have them do it. There's too many other fun things in life to do other than take a few days to plant a tree. And if you don't know what you're doing, and I can't tell you everything you need to know in a book, you might wear yourself out, hurt yourself, and still kill the tree.

Transplanting small trees is relatively easy, I mean a tree you can pick up with maybe a little help from someone else and move along in a wheel barrow. The same procedure can be used for hedges and shrubs.

If you're digging up a small tree, hedge or shrub for transplanting, first, gather all the tools you need to finish the job and have them ready. Next, without hesitation, buy *Soil Pro* and have it close by the hole you are going to plant into.

Some gardeners feel you should cut deep around your tree as much as a full month before you intend to move it.

They say get a sharpshooter and cut around the drip line. In doing this, you cut off the roots but smaller roots form and this allows them time to heal in their own environment to soften the blow of being moved.

Most of you, I know, won't do that. That's why I say get this Soil Pro ready because this will help your plant for those (like me) who want to dig and transplant in a single day. Be smart about this now, and follow what I tell you and I think your plant will survive.

I'd dig the hole that I plan to transplant my "growing thing" into at least as wide and as deep as a size-and-a-half of the root system of the item I'm planting. Then, dig another several inches more around that and 6 or 8 inches deeper. You want room for the new roots to take hold in the Soil Pro.

Then, go back to the plant you are digging and dig deep with a shovel or sharpshooter, making certain you get under the root system and break off as few roots as you can from the sides by digging just outside the drip line of the plant. Now, slip your shovel under the plant and cut off the roots that are trying to hold it secure.

TIP: My daddy used to take ordinary chicken wire and push it under the root ball as far as he could to keep the dirt intact, then wrap it around the root system and move it. I've used burlap to do the same thing.

If you're just moving the plant from one side of your lawn to the other, put it on a tarp or dropcloth and drag it slowly across the grass. If you have to put it in a wheel barrow to transport it a farther distance, just be careful not to drop it or roll it or lose to much dirt.

When you get to this new hole, start your preparation for a smooth transition. A good move might be to spread a tarp or dropcloth here too so you won't lose too much dirt in the grass, and mix in that Soil Pro 400 with this new dirt same as if you're making biscuits.

Then, fill the hole with water and watch it disappear as it seeps into the soil. Add several shovelsful of mix to the bottom of the hole, slip the plant in and fill the outer edges with the same mix, Soil Pro 400 and the dirt from the hole. Then, water it in.

There's no need to use peat moss, compost, cow manure, root stimulator or anything else except that mixture. The watering when the plant is in the hole helps remove air pockets and brings the root system against the new soil mixture. Then, ordinary care and your plant will grow.

If you're bringing home a container plant from a nursery, use the same planting procedure, it'll work each and every time. Just make certain that yyoucut the flimsy container with pruning shears and handle the roots gently.

Most plants in a container might have roots flush against the side and/or circling the plant, so dig the hole wide enough to spread out the roots and follow with this Soil

Pro/soil mixture. If the tree is burlaped, plant it "as is" but cut around the top of the burlap and let the bottom and sides contain the original soil. In time, the burlap will disintegrate.

There truly is so much to tell and I might be just touching the tip of the iceberg here but if you're not certain about any of this, call the program or what? Ask the nursery people where you purchased the tree, bush, or shrub. They're there to help.

BUILDING A COMPOST BIN

First, you had better live in the country or have a mighty big back yard before you do this because it isn't always necessarily kind to your neighbors. Compost is not a secret mixture and most people know it's a combination of grass, leaves, almost any kind of manure you can find and some garbage. It just so happens that the right mixture is healthy for your garden.

A simple compost pile is to dig a hole maybe a foot deep and five by five foot square then start layering it in, coat the bottom with four or so inches of leaves, throw a little dirt back in over it, add some fertilizer (12-24-12) or whatever you have in the garage and sprinkle it down. Then add another layer until the pile is filled.

About once a month, take the pruning fork and dig deep and turn it over and expose it to the air. I'd say hose the entire mess down with Medina. It will promote the bacteria to where it produces humus...that black, foul smelling dirt. Perfect for flower beds and all plants.

For a larger pile (if you have the room) I built four frames of treated 2 x 4's, 4 feet high and 6 feet long and nailed some hog wire to it with staples. I used treated 1 by 4's as cross braces then nailed two pairs of them together making two "L's". Then, with ordinary door latches, the kind that slip into an eyelet, I stood them up, latched them together and I had a solid box - my compost bin. To get to it easy, I just unlatch a couple of latches and it opens.

I toss in my leaves and fertilizer and anything else that will rot, like banana peels, egg shells, orange skins, and mix it up. Again, this is good for large yards or rural homes. If you live in the city, the best way is to buy the products you need from Medina, Soil Pro, Easy Gro or a mixture of what you need from your nursery and put it in a plastic container the size of a very large garbage can.

If you have a small front yard and/or patio, buy the stuff ready made and ready mixed as you need it but if you have a home and you get into planting, you'll want a large can or two of this around for planting new flowers or for transplanting.

I know I must have left out a thousand things that you wanted to know about. I tried to cover as many as I could, but darn if I didn't run out of energy and this book is over. Most new writers, I'm told, try to put everything they know into their first book but I'm just plumb tuckered out and will save more to say in upcoming books.

I enjoy it all, ladies and gentlemen, friends and neighbors, relatives and golfing partners. I mean I like planting things, talking about them, helping people and feeling a bit important while doing it.

If you learned anything from this book or enjoyed some of the humor and stories, call the program and tell me about it. If you have a suggestion, I'll take those into consideration for my next book. If you have a negative comment or criticism, like Archie told Edith, "Stifle yourself." If you think it's easy, you try writing one of these things.

Here I go, messin' with your head again. The truth is, I tried hard to be both informative, down-to-earth and even a bit funny. I'm an ordinary country boy but older than a boy. I am ordinary though and I'm certainly country so I had best be movin' up the road a piece to get my corn bread, turnip greens and hog jowls.

Don't forget, once a month **KTRH** has their *Yard of the Month* contest and we ask for pictures of your front yard, we choose which ones look best then go out and visit these front yards. We'll take our Yard of the Month sign out to the winner and also give them some neat prizes such as, a Snapper, self-propelled, mulching lawn mower, $300 of Medina products, and the Ortho problem solver book, valued at $225. Well, that's the prizes for this month, I think they vary so don't hold me to this.

The winner gets to keep the sign, and they can leave it up forever. We have not given a prize to anyone who has a fence in their front yard, so keep that in mind. Enjoy your gardening, keep those calls coming in to *GardenLine* and if I can help, just ask. Good luck and God bless.

MEET THE AUTHOR

Let me tell you about the man, John Burrow. He claims to be younger than most former Presidents of the United States. He was born in Tulia, Texas, fifty miles south of Amarillo, on a 160 acre cotton and maize rented farm. He attended grammar and high school there in Tulia and when he graduated, instead of going into college, he joined the U.S. Navy in 1962. His first choice was the Air Force but the navy recruiter was the only one who called him back.

John was a big boy; at 15 he was over six feet tall and weighed 200 pounds. Since then, he has grown a few more inches and gained an additional 40 or so pounds. His easy-going demeanor reminds you of John Wayne and his eyes have a sparkle in them. He doesn't smile much; he says he has a low upper lip that covers his top teeth and his smile shows only lower teeth.

While in the navy for four years, John was a hospital corpsman and worked in anesthesiology. This could have been the beginning of his career in radio. He is so low-key and so relaxed it seems that he is *still* involved with anesthesiology or some of that stuff soaked in his skin. I don't mean that he lulls his listeners to sleep, but he has a slow, easy way about him that makes you listen to each word.

Then came a variety of jobs that John prefers not to mention other than he sold new and used cars, worked as a bartender, and at road construction. His first radio show was on KGNC in Amarillo from 1974 to 1986 where he did the Farm and Ranch report. *"Cows and Plows,"* he calls it. *"I talked about hogs and cattle, horses and hay, feed and manure, and corn and cotton."*

John traveled all over the country talking about agriculture, as far north as Canada and as far west as Hawaii. In May of 1986 he got a call from KTRH to team up with Bill Zak on GardenLine.

*"Our show was on from 4 to 6 **AM** and I had lots of free time to learn about gardening. I audited the Master Gardeners Course, I listened intently to whatever Bill said, read every garden book I could get my hands on and I studied on my own. I went to meetings on flowers and plants and grass, and read every pamphlet and brochure published. I also spent a lot of time at nurseries and talking to nurserymen (and women), attended seminars on herbicides, fungicides, pesticides and fertilizer. I often stop in at nurseries who advertise on our show and meet the owners and/or managers and they share good tips with me.*

"I learn a lot from those who advertise on the show. We look over what we advertise and we don't advertise junk. These new formulas for proper plant growth are the very best. I know that grandad and grandma had their way of planting and growing things and I respect that, but modern technology is so advanced that the "old" way might have been the best then, but, trust the fact, the "new" way is the best now."

John is a husband, a father and a golfer, not necessarily in that order. If the weather is bad, he's a husband and a father. If the weather is good, he's a golfer. He's a sports fan too, and loves both the Oilers and the Cowboys. He feared a Texas Super Bowl, not knowing where his true allegiance would lie.

"Guess it would have to be with the Oilers. Houston is my home and the Oilers are my team. But, now that it's decided, How about them Cowboys? Super Bowl champs two years running."

Editor

USEFUL NUMBERS

ARIENS Lawn mowers . . . . (512) 863-2998
Big State Pest Contol . . . .(713) 667-3787
Champion Top Soil . . . . (713) 558-9948
Covington Nursery . . .(Dan Loep) . . . . . . (713) 447-1690
Department of Entomology, Texas A&M . . (409) 845-6800
Easy Gro (ESCO) . . . . (713) 864-7771
Fosters Tree Service . . . . (713) 458-5992
Galveston Orchid society . . . . (409) 948-3393
Harris County Extension Agent . . . . (713) 855-5600
Houston Orchid society . . . . (713) 320-8005
KTRH (Main Switchboard) . . . . (713) 526-KTRH
KTRH GardenLine (Houston area) . . . . . . (713) 526-4740
KTRH (Long Distance) . . . . (713) 630-5740
KTRH (Mobile) . . . . (713) STAR-4-740
Medina Home & Garden Products . . . . . . (210) 426-3011
Mercer Aboretum . . . . (713) 443-8731
Ortho Product Information 1-800 225-2883
Ortho Emergency line (24 hours) 1-800 424-9300
Paul's Precious Pecans 1-800 352-4061
RCW Nursery (Tom or Doris Williamson) . (713) 440-5161
Soil Pro . . . . (713) 893-8088. . .1-800-829-0215
Texas Poison Control . . . . (713) 654-1701

GardenLine Book YOUR FRONT YARD by John Burrow
(Houston area) . . . . (713) 268-6776
(Long Distance) 1-800 KTRH-740

INDEX

133

Oh no! You can't get away just yet. I have some terrific quotes to share with you, ones I hope you enjoy.

On laughter: "Laughter is the sun that drives winter from the human face."   Victor Hugo

On humor: "There are very few good judges of humor, and they don't agree."   Josh Billings

On trees: "Woodman, spare that tree! Touch not a single bow! In youth it sheltered me. And I'll protect it now." George P. Morris - Woodman, Spare That Tree.

On books: "Some said John, print it, others said Not so; Some said, It might be good, others said, No." Bunyan - Apology for his book

On flowers: "Flowers are the beautiful hieroglyphics of nature, with which she indicates how much she loves us." Goeth

On plants: "All animals on our planet (including us) are guests of the plant kingdom. No plants, equal no people or animals. It's that simple."   Malcolm C. Shurtleffp

JOHN BURROW is available for personal appearances, luncheons, banquets, home shows, seminars, etc. He is entertaining and informative. Call (713) 388-2547 for cost and availability.

For a copy(s) of *YOUR FRONT YARD* by John Burrow, send a personal check or money order in the amount of $12.85 for each book to:

SWAN PUBLISHING
126 Live Oak, Suite 100
Alvin, TX 77511

Please allow 7-10 days for delivery.

To order by Visa, MC, AMEX or Discover, call: (713) 268-6776 or long distance 1-800-KTRH-740.

LIBRARIES—BOOKSTORES—QUANTITY ORDERS
(713) 388-2547 or FAX (713) 585-3738